RESCUING MUSSOLINI

Gran Sasso 1943

ROBERT FORCZYK

First published in 2010 by Osprey Publishing
Midland House, West Way, Botley, Oxford OX2 0PH, UK
44–02 23rd St, Suite 219, Long Island City, NY 11101, USA
E-mail: info@ospreypublishing.com

Print ISBN: 978 1 84603 462 6
PDF e-book ISBN: 978 1 84908 275 4

Page layout by: Bounford.com, Cambridge, UK
Index by Alan Thatcher
Typeset in Sabon
Maps by Bounford.com, Cambridge, UK
3D BEVs by Alina Illustrazioni & Alan Gilliland
Originated by PPS Grasmere Ltd, Leeds, UK
Printed in China through Worldprint Ltd

10 11 12 13 14   10 9 8 7 6 5 4 3 2 1

A CIP catalog record for this book is available from the British Library

ACKNOWLEDGMENTS

I would like to thank Pier Paolo Battistelli for recommending Italian source
material, providing photographs from his collection, and proofreading
the manuscript for errors in Italian names. I would also like to thank
Monika Geilen from the Bundesarchiv for her prompt assistance in
assembling photographs.

DEDICATION

This volume is dedicated to Captain Cory J Jenkins and Captain John L
Hallett II, 1st Battalion/17th Infantry "Buffaloes," KIA in southern
Afghanistan, 25 September 2009.

ARTIST'S NOTE

Readers may care to note that the original paintings from which the color
plates in this book were prepared are available for private sale. All
reproduction copyright whatsoever is retained by the Publishers. All
inquiries should be addressed to:

Howard Gerrard
11 Oaks Road
Tenterden
Kent
TN30 6RD
UK

The Publishers regret that they can enter into no correspondence upon
this matter.

THE WOODLAND TRUST

Osprey Publishing are supporting the Woodland Trust, the UK's leading
woodland conservation charity, by funding the dedication of trees.

FOR A CATALOGUE OF ALL BOOKS PUBLISHED BY OSPREY MILITARY
AND AVIATION PLEASE CONTACT:

Osprey Direct, c/o Random House Distribution Center,
400 Hahn Road, Westminster, MD 21157
Email: uscustomerservice@ospreypublishing.com

Osprey Direct, The Book Service Ltd, Distribution Centre,
Colchester Road, Frating Green, Colchester, Essex, CO7 7DW
E-mail: customerservice@ospreypublishing.com

www.ospreypublishing.com

CONTENTS

INTRODUCTION

Raiding is a form of warfare that has existed since the dawn of human history and its essence remains to "hit-and-run" with a small, quick force before a larger opponent can react. In modern terms, raids are defined as short-duration tactical operations that are intended to achieve a specific purpose and either withdraw or hand off the mission to a larger relief force. Traditionally, raiding was a mission assigned to cavalry units since only they had the mobility to go after objectives deep in hostile territory and to evade decisive engagement by larger enemy forces. The main objective of such raids was usually limited to disrupting enemy lines of communication.

Despite the advent of mass armies in the 19th century, and the implicit belief that "God is always on the side of the big battalions," it gradually became apparent to Western military theorists by the turn of the 20th century that there were circumstances that required smaller, more specialized units. A series of British tactical defeats during the first phase of the Boer War from 1899 to 1900 resulted in the creation of the Lovat Scouts, Britain's first dedicated sniper unit. The "big battalions" continued to dominate the battlefield in the early stages of World War I, but the advent of trench warfare presented a conundrum that conventional infantry tactics could not resolve. In order to break enemy defensive lines their artillery had to be neutralized, but large-scale attacks by infantry units were usually decimated in "no man's land" and could not reach the hostile artillery. Gradually, both sides created specialized "trench raider" units to harass the enemy trench defenses, but they lacked the means to penetrate in depth. New tactics and new units were required.

The battlefield experiences of 1915–16 reinforced the general impression that conventional units were poorly suited for decentralized tactical operations and that elite units were best suited for raiding operations. In order to be considered elite, a military unit needs three things: specialized training, selective recruiting and superior equipment. Although the concept of elite units had existed for some time – mostly in terms of showpiece imperial guards units – the new tactics called for smaller company- and battalion-size units that would be built with specific missions in mind. The first elite special forces units began to appear in 1917, as the Italians created Arditi assault units and the Germans formed Stosstruppen units. Both types of units were formed from the best troops available and given special training in the new infiltration tactics. Officers and non-commissioned officers (NCOs) in these units were trained to operate independently and to use a high level of initiative. In addition, the development of light machine guns, mortars, and hand grenades made it possible

AUGUST 1941

Formation of Fallschirmjäger-Lehr Bataillon

1943

Formation of SS-Friedenthal Group

to give a company-size formation the firepower equivalent to a much larger unit. Using infiltration tactics, an elite raiding force now stood a decent chance of reaching the enemy's artillery line and other vital targets in their rear areas.

Although the Arditi and Stosstruppen units enjoyed a good deal of success in 1918, it was soon apparent that they lacked the mobility to strike anything beyond tactical targets. Technology again offered a potential solution with the development of effective parachutes, and the French actually managed to airdrop a few two-man sabotage teams behind German lines before the end of World War I. However, airborne units did not become a practical reality until the Soviet Union conducted extensive airborne maneuvers in 1935 and 1936, including the first use of combat gliders. Germany responded by forming the 7.Flieger-Division in 1938 and began developing the DFS-230 glider.

Vertical assault was still just a theory when World War II began, but it was quickly vindicated by the successful German airborne operation against Norway in April 1940 and then the glider/airborne attacks on Belgium and Holland the following month. These operations demonstrated that elite units could use vertical assaults to successfully conduct raids that could not otherwise be accomplished by larger conventional units. Flushed by their success in 1940, the Germans attempted five more glider assaults in Greece and Crete in 1941 against better-defended targets but suffered heavy losses for limited success. In November 1941, the British demonstrated a new dimension to raiding when they used a submarine to insert a commando team to attack Rommel's headquarters in Libya; not only did the raid fail, but it was also revealed that Rommel had not been at this site for two weeks – indicating the critical dependence upon timely intelligence for successful deep penetration raids.

Even prior to their successful vertical assaults in 1940, the Germans had recognized the urgent need for covert reconnaissance units that could identify targets

JUNE 1943

Skorzeny takes command of SS-Friedenthal Group

A formation of the SS-Sonder Lehrgang zbv Friedenthal in mid-1943. The unit was set up as a rival to the Abwehr's Brandenburg Regiment but was intended primarily for sabotage and assassination missions rather than direct actions. (Bundesarchiv, Bild 101III-Alber-183-19, Fotograf: Kurt Alber)

far behind enemy lines, as well as conduct sabotage missions. At the start of World War II the Abwehr (German military intelligence) formed the Brandenburg Regiment, which was successfully used in clandestine missions supporting the invasions of Poland, Holland, Yugoslavia, and the Soviet Union. In turn, the British set up the SOE (Special Operations Executive) to conduct clandestine operations in occupied Europe, while the Commandos and the SAS/Long Range Desert Group (LRDG) were established to conduct specialized raids. When the United States entered the war, it set up the Office of Strategic Services (OSS) for clandestine operations and the Army Rangers for raiding. Although the Wehrmacht relied upon the Fallschirmjäger to provide raiding units and capabilities, the bureaucratic in-fighting within the Third Reich led to the SS setting up its own clandestine unit in early 1943, known as the Friedenthal Battalion.

By the end of 1942 virtually all the major combatants had formed some type of special unit for raiding missions, and the scope of the missions was changing from merely disrupting enemy lines of communications to going after heavily defended, high-value targets. During 1942, the British demonstrated the feasibility of Trojan-horse operations with the raid on St Nazaire in March and the use of small boats for a long-range penetration attack on the port of Bordeaux in December. By 1943, raids by special forces had evolved to the point where a carefully planned operation stood a decent chance of neutralizing even some of the best-protected targets. However, hostage rescue was not a standard mission at the time and even the few attempts to target specific enemy commanders had failed due to inadequate intelligence. It was clear that in order to have good prospects for success, a raid had to be carefully planned and conducted by a well-trained force with combat experienced leaders.

THE SS-FRIEDENTHAL GROUP

In the Byzantine politics of the Third Reich, the SS – which already controlled domestic intelligence by means of the Gestapo and SD – had long been looking for a means to take over the foreign intelligence role from the Abwehr, run by Admiral Wilhelm Canaris. One of the Abwehr's few coups had been the creation of the covert action Brandenburg Regiment in 1939. After witnessing the Brandenburgers win renown during 1940–42, Himmler was eager to develop a similar-type unit for his SS.

In early 1942, Himmler's chief of staff, Gruppenführer Hans Jüttner, ordered the establishment of a "special training course" at the SS barracks in Oranienburg (which was adjacent to the Sachsenhausen concentration camp), some 30 kilometers north of Berlin. The unit, originally consisting of 100 SS men, was administered by the RSHA's Dept 6 (Foreign Intelligence). A Dutch officer, SS-Hauptsturmführer

Pieter van Vessem, was selected to command the unit, which was initially called Sonder Lehrgang Oranienburg. The "special training" consisted of espionage, sabotage, and limited parachute training (for individuals, not mass drops). Efforts to insert SS-trained agents into Ireland and Persia both failed.

After accomplishing nothing in its first year, the unit moved into an old hunting lodge in Friedenthal, near Oranienburg, and was redesignated SS-Sonder Lehrgang zbv Friedenthal. By early 1943 the unit expanded as more volunteers came from Dutch SS groups and Volksdeutsch from other countries. A number of volunteers also came from the SD, bored concentration-camp guards and men from the SS-Einsatzgruppen in Eastern Europe (who were required to complete a combat tour of duty and preferred a unit stationed near Berlin to an SS division on the Eastern Front). Frustrated by the fumbling start to SS "special forces," Walter Schellenberg sought new leadership and decided to replace Vessem with Otto Skorzeny. Although assigned in late April 1943, Skorzeny did not actually arrive to take command of the unit until June 1943, which was then redesignated SS-Jäger-Bataillon 502. Skorzeny brought a number of Austrian Nazi cronies with him, such as SS-Obersturmführer Karl Radl, as well as associates from his vehicle-repair battalion, such a SS-Untersturmführer Ulrich Menzel.

Schellenberg authorized Skorzeny to recruit soldiers from the Wehrmacht as well as the SS and by the time of Mussolini's overthrow, the unit had about 350 personnel. However, the unit was a battalion in name only, since it was not trained to fight as a cohesive group but to operate as small, dispersed clandestine teams, often in civilian clothes. Training emphasis was on covert reconnaissance, sabotage, and assassination, not infantry tactics. Despite later descriptions of "SS-Commandos," the Friedenthal troops were never trained or equipped as a combat assault unit. Skorzeny himself had very little combat experience and most of the officers he picked for the unit were no better: Radl had been a paper-pusher in the SD's political intelligence section; SS-Untersturmführer Robert Warger (another Austrian Nazi) had only served in the SD; and Menzel had seen some action with the SS-Reich Division in 1941, but as a medical platoon leader. Warger was so short and slight of frame that he had been rejected for frontline service. Indeed, by mid-1943 the Germans were beginning to comb out their rear echelon units for infantry replacements; the best material went to the frontline Waffen-SS units in Russia while Skorzeny had to make do with whatever was left. He even received replacements from the Kriegsmarine, such as Untersturmführer Hans Mändel, who transferred to the Friedenthal group from a naval flak unit. Of the officers Skorzeny took with him to Italy, only SS-Untersturmführer Otto Schwerdt and SS-Untersturmführer Andreas Friedrich had any real prior combat experience. Schwerdt had fought as an NCO in the SS-Totenkopf Division's pioneer battalion

during 1940–41 and received both the Iron Cross 1st and 2nd Class. Friedrich had also fought in the SS-Reich Division in the Yelnya Bridgehead in August 1941, where he was wounded and awarded the Iron Cross 1st Class. However, the general lack of combat experience and combat training showed during the Gran Sasso raid, where most of Skorzeny's men were next to useless in storming the hotel.

In his memoirs, Skorzeny described the NCOs he took to Italy as "the pick of the litter," but judging by the records of his NCOs, this wasn't saying much. SS-Unterscharführer Hans Holzer was one of the few with considerable combat experience, having served as a machine-gunner with the SS-Totenkopf Division in the West and Russian campaigns and being awarded both the Iron Cross 1st and 2nd Class. Yet Holzer was far from typical of Skorzeny's NCOs and he took a number of men with him that had just transferred into the unit from rear-area duties. For example, SS-Unterscharführer Bernhard Cieslewitz had joined the SS only five months before the raid and was trained as a mechanic.

Even after the Gran Sasso raid, the Friedenthal group did not become a commando-type unit but remained focused on unconventional warfare. Shortly after Gran Sasso, Skorzeny sent Schwerdt, Holzer and several new recruits to Denmark to conduct a counter-resistance operation that was eventually dubbed "the Peters Group." In 16 months, Schwerdt's group was responsible for the assassination of 102 Danes suspected of involvement with the resistance, as well as numerous acts of arson and sabotage that resulted in civilian deaths. After the war, Schwerdt was sentenced to death in Copenhagen, but released from prison in 1953. Far from being commandos, the Friedenthal group was best suited for terror and sabotage missions against occupied civilian populations, rather than combat assault against real soldiers.

ORIGINS

Kidnapping Mussolini

Hitler met with Mussolini near Salzburg, Austria on April 7–11, 1943. Although relations between them were beginning to strain due to the deteriorating Axis position in Russia and North Africa, Hitler still regarded Mussolini as his only real ally. For his part, Mussolini recognized that the war was going against them and urged Hitler to negotiate an armistice with the Soviets in order to concentrate their efforts against the Western Allies. (Bundesarchiv, Bild 183-B23938, Fotograf: Gerhard Baatz)

By the summer of 1943 Benito Mussolini, dictator of Fascist Italy for over 20 years, was in a great deal of trouble. Since joining Germany as a co-belligerent in 1940, Italy had stumbled from one military setback to another, culminating with the destruction of the Italian 8th Army in Russia in January 1943, the loss of all Italian troops in North Africa in May 1943, and the Allied landings in Sicily on July 9, 1943. Rather than rallying to defend their native soil, Italian military morale was on the verge of collapse and it was clear that it was only a matter of time before Sicily and southern Italy were under Allied control. Even before the Allied landings in Sicily, members of Mussolini's own family, the military, and the government had been conspiring to replace him in order to seek an armistice with the Allies. These conspiratorial plans simmered for months but they became more serious after the Allied invasion of Sicily and then the first major Allied bombing raid on Rome itself on July 19, which killed about 1,500 civilians. Naples was bombed the next day, making it clear that Italy must get out of the war before the country faced a real catastrophe. The biggest obstacle to the conspirators was Mussolini himself, who remained wedded to his alliance with Hitler.

The anti-Mussolini conspiracy included members of the Comando Supremo (military high command), including its chief, Generale Vittorio Ambrosio, his

assistant, Generale di brigata Giuseppe Castellano and military police chief Generale di brigata Saverio Polito. Early on, the conspirators decided to rely upon the carabinieri (military police) to arrest Mussolini, since some members of the army were still loyal to the Italian dictator. However, by chance the Allied air raid on Rome killed the head of the carabinieri, Generale di brigata Azzolino Hazon, who was a key player in the conspiracy. Hurriedly, the conspirators connived to replace Hazon with Generale di corpo Angelo Cerica, who agreed to arrest Mussolini if the king authorized it. The conspirators also gained the tacit support of the civil *polizia*, under Carmine Senise and the elite Grenadiers of Sardinia under Generale di Divisione Giunio Ruggiero. Aware that the Allies could land in southern Italy at any time, the conspirators planned to arrest Mussolini on or about July 26 and occupy key points in Rome.

After a tempestuous meeting with his Fascist Grand Council on July 24, in which even the Duce's son-in-law Galeazzo Ciano voted against him, Mussolini went to meet with King Victor Emmanuelle III at his residence in the northern suburbs of Rome the next afternoon. Mussolini expected the king to side with him and help weed the conspirators out of the government. Instead, the king stunned Mussolini by informing him that "my dear Duce, there's no point going on. Italy is on her knees, the army has been completely defeated and the soldiers no longer want to fight for you. At this moment, you are the most hated man in Italy." The king then tersely stated that he was replacing Mussolini as prime minister with Maresciallo Pietro Badoglio.

When Mussolini tried to leave, he was put under arrest by six armed carabinieri officers led by Capitano Paolo Vigneri and driven off in an ambulance. Three hours later, the king announced Mussolini's resignation over the radio and those Fascists still loyal to Mussolini were caught by surprise. Detachments of carabinieri and *polizia* moved to seize key communications centers and arrest Mussolini's adherents, which prevented any counter-coup. Rather than rallying to their leader, most Fascists went into hiding or left the country (including Mussolini's own son Vittorio) and it was soon clear that the Duce's departure met with widespread approval. Crowds in Rome toppled statues of the dictator, attacked Fascist offices and shouted, "Death to Mussolini!"

Once Mussolini was out of the picture, Badoglio opted to maintain the façade of continuing the alliance with Germany, but covertly dispatched officers to neutral Portugal to begin negotiating an armistice with the Allies. Fearful of Hitler's response to the coup, the conspirators decided to keep Mussolini incommunicado until after negotiations were completed and the Allies had arrived in Rome, to prevent German retribution. The conspirators also decided to place Mussolini's wife, Rachele, his 15-year-old son, Romano, and 13-year-old daughter, Anna Maria, under house arrest. General Polito escorted Rachele to Mussolini's estate at Rocca delle Caminate, about 200km north of Rome, on August 3.[1] Polito instructed the *polizia* officers guarding them that if either Rachele or the children attempted to leave, to shoot them. Even Clara Pettaci, Mussolini's mistress, was eventually put under arrest although, in a display of pettiness, the Badoglio regime made a point of revealing her relationship with Mussolini to the press.

Hitler's decision

Adolf Hitler was at the Wolfsschanze headquarters near Rastenberg in East Prussia when the first reports about Mussolini's disappearance were received. Although Hitler had long admired Mussolini and had met with him only a week earlier on July 19, he was aware that defeatism was sapping Italy's will to continue fighting. In Hitler's paranoid mind nothing aroused greater fury than treachery, and upon learning of Mussolini's overthrow he immediately resolved to recover his ally and to crush those who had betrayed the Axis. He said, "This is real treason. I want the Duce to come immediately to Germany. I think we should have the 3.Panzergrenadier-Division immediately occupy Rome and arrest the whole government, the whole mob . . ."

However, the Oberkommando der Wehrmacht (OKW ["High Command of the Armed Forces"]) staff quickly informed Hitler that there were too few German troops to mount an immediate counter-coup in Rome and such a move could result in having to fight the 60,000 Italian troops around the capital. Instead, Hitler was persuaded that more German divisions should be sent to Italy before any overt moves against the conspirators should be conducted. He agreed to bide his time until there were sufficient German troops in Italy to mount Operation *Achse* (*Axis*), which would arrest the conspirators and disarm any disloyal Italian military units. However, Hitler

**JULY 24
1943**

Mussolini arrested

**JULY 26
1943**

**Hitler orders
Mussolini's rescue**

---

1 After Mussolini's rescue, Polito was later charged by the Fascist RSI regime with trying to seduce Rachele while she was in his custody.

was unwilling to sit by and allow Mussolini to be handed over to the Allies for trial, as this might encourage anti-Nazi conspirators in Germany. By the midday conference on July 26, the Führer decided to establish a special task force to find and then rescue Mussolini. Hermann Goring, eager to promote his own Luftwaffe capabilities, recommended General der Fallschirmtruppe Kurt Student's (Commanding General of Paratroops) Fliegerkorps XI headquarters, which was training in southern France. Remembering earlier airborne coups such as Eben Emael in 1940, Hitler reportedly said, "Splendid! He is the right man for this sort of thing."

Student was immediately ordered to Rastenberg, where Hitler ordered him to begin organizing the rescue operation; Hitler declared, "one of your special assignments will be to find and free my friend Mussolini." The rescue mission was designated Operation *Eiche* (*Oak*). Hitler also tasked Student with seizing control of Rome at the right moment and arresting the key conspirators, including the king and Badoglio. To assist Student in the search for Mussolini, the OKW had ordered several officers from the Abwehr's Brandenburg Battalion and Luftwaffe special units to report to Rastenberg. SS-Reichsführer Heinrich Himmler, who was also at Rastenberg, was not going to let all the credit go to his rivals Admiral Canaris and Goring, so he recommended a role for his SS troops as well.[2] SS-Hauptsturmführer Otto Skorzeny, commander of SS-Jäger-Bataillon 502, was ordered to Rastenberg and Himmler succeeded in convincing Hitler to select Skorzeny over the more qualified Brandenburg officers. Skorzeny was assigned to Student to conduct a covert search in Italy to identify Mussolini's location, as well as to assist in preparations to kidnap Badoglio and the king as part of Operation *Axis*. Although the Abwehr would also be involved in the search, Skorzeny was not instructed to coordinate his efforts with them. Hitler directed that these operations would be conducted under maximum security and that Student was not to inform Generalfeldmarschall Albert Kesselring (Oberbefehlshaber Süd/Commander-in-Chief South) or any other local German commanders in Italy about these covert operations.

In ordering this operation, Hitler's intent was based upon three questionable assumptions: that the coup was the work of only a handful of conspirators and that the Fascist party and the military still stood behind Mussolini; that, if rescued, Mussolini would be the same kind of leader-figure that he had been for 20 years: and that he could keep Italy in the war at Germany's side. Hitler made this decision after receiving only fragmentary initial reports from Rome but, as more information came in, it became apparent that the Fascist party had virtually disintegrated upon hearing of Mussolini's ousting and that neither the Italian people nor their military would lift a finger to save the Duce.

Preparations for Operation *Axis*

In order to address the larger problem of Italian defection, Hitler commanded Kesselring to begin detailed planning to implement Operation *Axis* to seize Rome by force and to disarm disloyal Italian military forces. Within days, the OKW directed four German infantry divisions to begin moving into northern Italy, with more reinforcements en route. Sensing that the Germans would strike, the Italian Comando Supremo sought to delay the German reinforcements as much as possible, playing for time while they were negotiating an armistice with the Allies.

---

2 KG 200 had a special-operations *staffel* that was trained in parachute operations, including sabotage and reconnaissance.

General der Fallschirmtruppe Kurt Student, commander of Fliegerkorps XI, tasked by Hitler with finding and rescuing Mussolini. Student had gained invaluable experience in planning and conducting both glider and parachute assaults during the campaigns in Holland and Crete. (Author's Collection)

Initially, the only significant German unit near Rome at the time of Mussolini's overthrow was the 3.Panzergrenadier-Division, located 95km south of the capital. The OKW immediately ordered the 2.Fallschirmjäger-Division to fly into the Pratica di Mare airbase from southern France and it began arriving in late July. Both divisions were recently formed formations and not fully manned or equipped, but they were reckoned to be a match for the six Italian divisions based around Rome. Student decided to co-locate his Fliegerkorps XI headquarters with Kesselring's headquarters in Frascati, southeast of Rome. Although Student did not overtly inform Kesselring of his true mission, Kesselring was soon aware that an effort was afoot to find Mussolini. As a security measure, Student and his staff referred to planning for Operation *Oak* under the codename "Bruno Meyer." However, Hitler's secrecy rule complicated the search effort to find Mussolini, since none of Kesselring's German forces scattered across Italy could be tasked to assist with locating the missing dictator. Furthermore, Student knew that Kesselring would need to use the bulk of the 2.Fallschirmjäger-Division for Operation *Axis*, potentially limiting the resources available for a rescue mission.

OTTO SKORZENY – "REAR AREA COMMANDO"

Otto Skorzeny's role in Operation *Oak* has been distorted by lingering remnants of Nazi propaganda and Skorzeny's own memoirs, which he used to enhance his image as "the most dangerous man in Europe." In fact, before Operation *Oak*, Skorzeny was an obscure SS officer who was sitting out most of the war "in the rear, with the gear," as they say.

Born in Vienna in 1908, his family was sufficiently well off for him to attend the University of Vienna, from which he graduated with a degree in engineering in 1931. While at university, he became active in right-wing politics and joined the Austrian Nazi party. He married after graduation and later claimed to have taken his honeymoon in the Abruzzi region of Italy, near the Gran Sasso. After six years in a minor engineering business in Vienna, Skorzeny became involved in the Austrian Anschluss of 1938 and, in his memoirs made several bombastic claims about his supposedly key role. At the start of World War II Skorzeny immediately volunteered for service in the Luftwaffe, unrealistically expecting to be commissioned and made a pilot, but instead serving as an ordinary Flieger (private) in a Luftwaffe Signal Replacement Regiment in Vienna until January 31, 1940.

Disappointed with the Luftwaffe, Skorzeny used some of his Nazi party connections to get a transfer to the Waffen-SS in February 1940, where he served three months as an SS-Schütze (private) in the SS-Leibstandarte's 2nd Reserve Replacement Battalion in Berlin-Lichterfelde. On May 1, 1940, Skorzeny was promoted to Unterscharführer and transferred to the Heavy Battalion (15cm) of the artillery regiment in the SS-Totenkopf Division, where he served as a mechanic for four months. Although the division saw considerable action in Belgium and France, Skorzeny only heard gunfire in the distance and did not receive the Iron Cross or any other combat awards. On September 1, 1940 Skorzeny was promoted to Oberscharführer and transferred to the artillery regiment in the SS-Reich Division.

Skorzeny continued to work his Nazi party contacts and on January 30, 1941 he was finally promoted to SS-Untersturmführer (Leutnant) in the SS-Reserve and assigned as a technical officer to the II Battalion in the Reich Division's artillery regiment. He served during the invasion of Yugoslavia in April 1941 and claimed to have single-handedly captured a number of Yugoslav soldiers (not coroborated in his SS records). Afterwards, Skorzeny was promoted to SS-Obersturmführer and he continued to serve with the SS-Reich Division in the opening stages of

Operation *Barbarossa*, although he was still primarily involved with supervising vehicle repairs. He was awarded the Iron Cross, 2nd Class on August 26, 1941 for vehicle recovery under fire during the fighting in the Yelnya Bridgehead. Sometime after the failure of Operation *Typhoon* in December 1941, Skorzeny became ill with stomach colic – a common occurrence for German soldiers during the first winter on the Eastern Front – and he was evacuated to Germany in January 1942. Although some poorly researched accounts suggest that Skorzeny was severely wounded by Soviet artillery fire, his SS records do not indicate any wound badges for that time and even he cites colic in his memoirs.

After recovering, Skorzeny was assigned to the SS Vehicle Replacement Battalion in Weimar-Buchenwald, where he spent the next eight months as an instructor on vehicle repair. Normally, sick or wounded officers returned to their parent divisions and the fact that Skorzeny did not indicates that he was not missed. Indeed, he had already acquired a reputation as a soldier with poor discipline and a big mouth. He never really lost the beer-hall mannerisms that had endeared him to his Austrian Nazi party comrades but which reflected poorly on a professional officer. In November 1942 Skorzeny was transferred to the newly formed Panzer Regiment of the SS-Totenkopf Division, where he spent the next four months getting their vehicles in shape but was then sent back to his old instructor slot.

While the Wehrmacht was fighting desperately in Russia in 1942–43, Skorzeny spent much of that time in the cafés of Berlin, networking with other Nazis. His efforts paid off when his old friend Ernst Kaltenbrunner (the former head of the Austrian Nazi party) was promoted to chief of the SS-Reichssicherheitshauptamt (RSHA) in early 1943. Kaltenbrunner arranged for Skorzeny to be offered a command in Walter Schellenberg's Amt.-VI of the SD. On April 28, 1943, Skorzeny was promoted to SS-Hauptsturmführer and transferred to take command of the SS-Oranienburg Special Training unit. He went through a basic Abwehr course on espionage but did not receive parachute or any other combat training. Although Skorzeny later claimed to have "intensely" studied British Commando methods during the summer of 1943, he actually spent more time socializing. Indeed, his staff had difficulty tracking him down when the call came during the middle of a duty day on July 26, 1943 for him to report directly to the Führer's headquarters – Skorzeny, in fact, was in civilian clothes drinking with some Austrian Nazi cronies on the Kurfürstendamm.

Skorzeny was chosen because of his party connections, despite his very limited combat experience and special skills. He saw the Friedenthal command as a chance to get a promotion, gain some recognition from his superiors, and be his own man, not to conduct suicidal, high-risk assignments. After the Gran Sasso raid, Skorzeny's reputation as a "commando extraordinaire" was created by SS propagandists to help boost Himmler's standing in the Nazi hierarchy. Once the Brandenbergers were reduced to a conventional role in 1944, Skorzeny inherited a number of skilled special forces soldiers from their ranks, such as Leutnant Baron Adrian von Fölkersam, whom Skorzeny made his adjutant and de facto operations officer, relieving himself of the burdens of actually running a military outfit.

(Getty Images)

However Skorzeny's record after Gran Sasso was mostly one of failure, not success. Plots to kidnap General de Gaulle or to assassinate the Big Three at the Tehran Conference came to nothing, and the effort to capture or kill Tito resulted in the virtual destruction of the SS-Fallschirmjäger Battalion 500. Indeed, Skorzeny's only post-Italy success was Operation *Panzerfaust* on October 15–16, 1944 in which he kidnapped the Hungarian regent's son and with a German armored column bluffed his way into the Budapest citadel. Skorzeny's coup, while bold, was tactically amateurish and crude, and, despite minimal Hungarian resistance, required crucial assistance from other Wehrmacht units – with whom he did not share the credit. For his coup in Budapest, Skorzeny was awarded the Deutsches Kreuz in Gold (DkiG) and promoted to Obersturmbannführer.

After Budapest, it was all downhill for Skorzeny and his SS special forces. His unit's unconventional role in the December 1944 Ardennes offensive, Operation *Greif*, briefly caused confusion behind American lines but it failed to achieve its objectives and most of the reconnaissance teams were captured. The rest of Skorzeny's reinforced regimental-size Kampfgruppe, dubbed Panzer Brigade 150, was then committed as a conventional unit to the Malmedy sector. Skorzeny had no idea how to mount a brigade-size attack and his unit was repulsed by the American 30th Infantry Division with heavy losses. When he was slightly wounded by shrapnel from American artillery fire, he claimed that Hitler had ordered him not to risk capture and turned over command of the brigade to his subordinates, returning to Berlin.

By early 1945 Germany no longer had the means to conduct special operations and when Himmler assumed command of Army Group Vistula in January 1945, he ordered Skorzeny to

take his remaining troops and set up a bridgehead at the town of Schwedt on the Oder. Skorzeny, now a Standartenführer, pulled together an *ad hoc* division-size Kampfgruppe composed of SS, Volksgrenadier and Luftwaffe remnants to hold the town. No major attempt to take the town was made and Skorzeny alienated Himmler (who had never liked him), and was relieved of command on February 28, 1945. Returning to Berlin, Skorzeny was ordered in mid-March to organize frogman attacks on the recently captured Ludendorff Bridge at Remagen, but these accomplished nothing. Despite this record of failure, Hitler admired Skorzeny for his loyalty to the Nazi cause and awarded him the Oak Leaves to his Ritterkreuz on April 9, 1945, for his role at Schwedt. Yet Skorzeny was not so loyal that he wished to remain with Hitler in Berlin to the end, and claimed to be headed to Bavaria to help organize Himmler's Werwolf partisan operations despite the fact that the Reichsführer had already decided to cancel this program. Skorzeny succeeded in bluffing his way out of a doomed Berlin and headed south with his old cohort, Karl Radl. Abandoning their men, Skorzeny and Radl sat out the last month of the war in a cozy mountain cottage in Bavaria, and then surrendered quietly to the Americans.

Skorzeny was a poor soldier, but he was an ardent Nazi and this political loyalty counted for more than professional skill. He was an accomplished and unabashed liar, comfortable with appropriating the deeds of others or shifting the blame for failure. It is also significant that Skorzeny's only operational successes were achieved against former allies who put up little or no resistance, rather than against well-armed enemies. After the war, Skorzeny continued to peddle the same exaggerations and falsehoods, which annoyed his wartime peers but which were often accepted by foreign journalists as fact.

INITIAL STRATEGY

The search for Mussolini

In order to rescue Mussolini, Student first had to find him, and that was no simple task. Tracking down a single individual who is being held incommunicado is one of the hardest assignments for any intelligence service, particularly when it has to be done inside an ostensibly allied country. Since the façade of alliance had to be maintained until Germany had the forces in Italy and the pretext to execute Operation *Axis*, German intelligence-collection operations had to be restrained in order not to precipitate any incidents. Further complicating the search, bureaucratic interaction between the Abwehr and the RSHA (Reichssicherheitshauptamt, Reich Security Head Office) was hostile and uncoordinated[3]. Hitler and Himmler also became personally involved in search operations, demanding frequent updates and adding their voices on the evaluation of information.

Initially, the German intelligence resources in Italy were clueless about Mussolini's whereabouts and could provide very little useful information to Student in order to begin planning a rescue. Shortly after the coup, the German ambassador in Rome met with King Victor Emmanuele III and Kesselring met with Badoglio, but neither was able to gain any useful details beyond the acknowledgement that Mussolini was being held in protective custody. Student assigned his intelligence officer, Hauptmann Gerhard Langguth, to begin setting up a search for Mussolini, while Skorzeny spent most of his time working out of the German embassy.

Two days after Hitler authorized the rescue mission, SS-Obersturmführer Karl Radl, adjutant of SS-Jäger-Bataillon 502, arrived with 29 personnel from the battalion at the Pratica di Mare airfield, 32km south of Rome. The SS men wore Luftwaffe tropical uniforms in order to maintain a low profile. Also attached to the Friedenthal detachment was a group of seven SD and three Gestapo officers under SS-Haupsturmführer Arno Besekow,[4] who were to assist in the search for Mussolini. Only Radl was given any information about the target; the rest of the SS men were given no mission details. Without any real idea of how to conduct a covert search operation, Skorzeny began sending out teams – most in civilian clothes – to scour Rome, looking at possible sites where Mussolini could be held, such as local carabinieri barracks. He gave his teams £5,000 in forged British currency for bribery purposes.[5] Predictably, having little idea what they were looking for, these young Germans, laden with cash, enjoyed a pleasant week of fraternizing in Rome. Italians proved quite willing to provide Skorzeny's men with complete fabrications, in return for wads of cash. Skorzeny's search effort was amateurish and produced nothing of intelligence value.

Himmler, who disapproved of Skorzeny from the start, ordered two more experienced SS officers stationed in Rome to assist in the search effort. SS-Sturmbannführer Herbert Kappler, who had been attached to the German embassy in Rome since 1939 as a liaison officer with the Italian police, would play a major role in the search. SS-Obersturmbannführer Eugen Dollmann, an Italophile RSHA liaison officer from Himmler's staff, would also play a significant role in the

---

3 Under SS-Obergruppenführer Dr Ernst Kaltenbrunner, this organization included the SD and Gestapo. Skorzeny's unit worked for Amt-VI (Department 6), foreign intelligence.
4 Besekow was involved with Einsatzgruppe "special actions" activities around Riga in 1941.
5 This was a product of Operation *Bernhard*, the SS-run counterfeit operation conducted at the Sachsenhausen concentration camp, right next to Skorzeny's Friedenthal headquarters.

search. Himmler ordered both officers to assist in Skorzeny's search efforts. This was a high-end/low-end HUMINT (Human Intelligence) operation, with Kappler using his extensive police contacts and informants while Dollmann mingled with Italian high society, seeking clues on Mussolini's location. Kappler's contacts with the Italian police soon revealed that after his arrest Mussolini had been held at a carabinieri barracks only 5 kilometers from Kesselring's headquarters. Although Mussolini had already been moved by the time Kappler received this information, further tips indicated that the Duce had been driven to the port of Gaeta by General Polito and then transferred by Italian corvette to a small island off the coast. While Langguth and Skorzeny were mulling over which island Mussolini might have been transferred to, Student was inundated with a steady stream of rumors from the Abwehr and other sources that the Duce was on Ventotene island, then Elba, then Santo Stefano, then in the port of La Spezia. Hitler demanded daily updates on the search and seized on each possible indicator as proof of Mussolini's location, forcing Student to expend his limited collection resources running down red herrings. Himmler also kept meddling with the search, since his RSHA assets were involved. By this point, the Italian Servizio Informazione Militare (SIM), now loyal to the Badoglio regime, was aware of German interest in Mussolini's location and was feeding a steady stream of disinformation to Kappler's informants. In fact, Mussolini spent July 28 to August 7 on the island of Ponza, which was not considered by the Germans.

Even though Mussolini was moved by an Italian destroyer to the island of La Maddalena near Sardinia on August 8, the cumbersome German search process had decided that he was located on the island of Santo Stefano. Student duly began planning an airborne raid on the island, including the use of Kriegsmarine light naval units for extraction. However, a veritable flood of other tips kept pouring in and the raid on Santo Stefano was put on hold. Langguth and Skorzeny gradually reoriented on La Maddalena island after several credible reports about the Duce's transfer were received. On a hunch, Skorzeny decided to send one of his Italian-speaking officers, SS-Untersturmführer Robert Warger, as a covert agent to La Maddalena to try and confirm whether or not Mussolini was there. Warger spent most of his time bar-hopping, picking up idle gossip, but eventually radioed Skorzeny that he had actually seen Mussolini (Warger's claim may have been exaggerated) at Villa Weber on the coast. Upon hearing this, Skorzeny decided to get a closer look at La Maddalena and he commandeered a light plane[6] to conduct a visual reconnaissance of the target area. Near the island, Skorzeny ordered the pilot to fly at very low altitude to get a good look at the target, but instead the pilot stalled the aircraft and belly-landed in the water. Skorzeny and the pilot survived the ditching and were ignominiously rescued by Italian sailors from the island. Upon returning to Frascati, Skorzeny convinced Student that Mussolini was on La Maddalena, who began planning a daring naval raid, using a company of his Fallschirmjäger and an S-Boote flotilla. Student and Skorzeny both flew to Rastenberg to brief Hitler on the impending La Maddalena raid. At this point Hitler commented that, since Italy and Germany were still allies, the rescue mission might be attributed to Italian Fascists, rather than to German paratroopers.

In any case, the German search efforts had not gone unnoticed by the Italians, and Badoglio ordered that Mussolini be moved off La Maddalena before the Germans could mount a rescue operation. Early on August 28, Mussolini was flown by seaplane to an airbase on Lake Bracciano, northwest of Rome, then driven by car to

---

6 Some sources state this was an He-111 bomber, but this is unlikely.

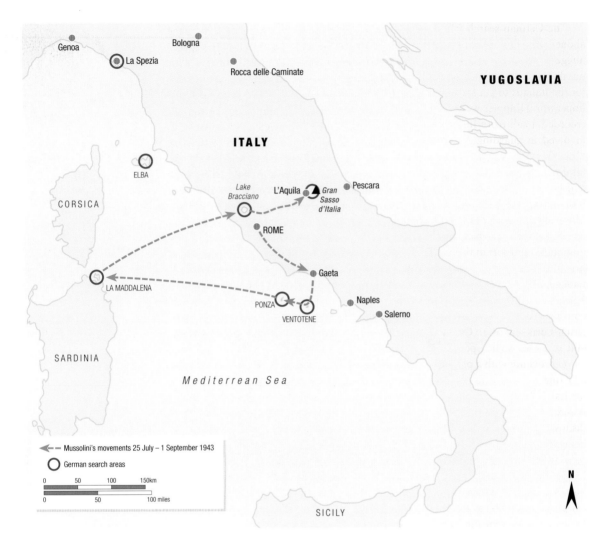

Mussolini's movements 25 July – 1 September 1943

○ German search areas

| 0 | 50 | 100 | 150km |

| 0 | 50 | 100 miles |

N

Mussolini's movements,
25 July–1 September 1943.

the village of Assergi in the eastern Abruzzi region. Four days later he was brought by cable car up to the Hotel Campo Imperatore[7] atop the Gran Sasso mountain range, which the carabinieri felt was isolated enough to preclude any rescue operation. Badoglio ordered the guard detachment to be reinforced and directed that Mussolini was not to fall into German hands alive.

Having decided that the target was La Maddalena, Skorzeny then made the incredibly amateurish decision to return to the island himself, accompanied by Warger and disguised as sailors. Although he had been provided with a team of RSHA agents trained in covert espionage, Skorzeny apparently wanted to grab any credit himself (and possibly thought that he could pull off an ad hoc snatch with just himself and one subordinate). Instead, he had barely arrived on the island when he heard from talkative Italian police that Mussolini had just been moved back to the mainland. In Rome, Dollmann was able to confirm this from high-level Italian contacts. Once again, the sudden transfer of Mussolini junked Student's tactical planning just before it reached fruition and the Germans temporarily lost track of where to look next.

---

7 The Hotel was also known as the Albergo Refugio, but the Germans referred to it as Hotel Campo Imperatore.

The German search effort again spewed out a stream of mostly useless rumors about Mussolini's possible new location, but it was Kappler who found the "golden nugget."[8] Using standard Gestapo methods, Kappler had installed wiretaps on a number of critical communication nodes in Rome and then just sat back and waited for the Italians to get sloppy. Shortly after Mussolini was transferred to the Campo Imperatore, Kappler was rewarded when his tap on the Ministry of Interior's phone recorded a call from Inspector General Giuseppe Gueli (who was suspected to be involved in guarding Mussolini) to chief of police Carmine Senise, which said, "Security precautions around the Gran Sasso complete." Kappler passed this vital information to Langguth and Skorzeny. The Germans were also aware that Mussolini had been transferred by seaplane, and Langguth checked on activity around the Italian seaplane base on Lake Bracciano, north of Rome. By chance, a Luftwaffe officer stationed near Lake Bracciano had noticed a seaplane arriving with an unusual level of security, which was passed on to Langguth. Student believed that a mountaintop resort in the Gran Sasso made sense as a hiding place for an important prisoner, but wanted more information before he could put together a rescue. Langguth suggested that Leutnant Leo Krutoff, a medical officer on the Fliegerkorps XI staff, could be sent to Gran Sasso ostensibly to check out the hotel as a possible convalescent site for German troops suffering from malaria. Student agreed and Krutoff was sent off to Gran Sasso on the morning of September 8. Langguth was also able to gather some open-source information about the possible target, including a travel brochure with a photo of the Hotel Campo Imperatore and a description from a German who had vacationed at the hotel before the war. In addition, Kappler sent his Italian-speaking deputy, SS-Obersturmführer Erich Priebke, to the area around Assergi and he found out that all the staff from the Hotel Campo Imperatore had been dismissed in early September, which seemed to indicate that someone important was being kept there.

Impatiently, Skorzeny demanded a reconnaissance flight over the hotel and Langguth accompanied him and Radl aboard an He-111 bomber. The flight was a bust because the internal cameras malfunctioned, but Skorzeny managed to get a couple of very poor-quality photos using a hand-held camera. Just as Skorzeny and Langguth were returning to Frascati at 1210 hours, 131 American B-17 bombers struck the town, intending to demolish Kesselring's headquarters just before the Salerno landings.[9] Amazingly, the Italians scrambled 30 fighters to intercept the raiders – the last major sortie flown by the Regia Aeronautica before the armistice was announced – but shot down only a single bomber. The American bombers flattened nearly half the town with 389 tons of bombs, killing 485 Italian civilians as well as about 150 Germans. Although Kesselring and his staff survived the raid, he decided to move his headquarters to Monte Soratte, north of Rome.

Since the Luftwaffe photo development facility at Frascati was destroyed in the air raid, Langguth and Skorzeny went to Pratica di Mare to develop the film from their early morning sortie. Unfortunately the photos revealed very little detail about the hotel or the surrounding terrain, since the hotel was only about a 2mm-wide blob on the 1:20,000-scale photo. However, there did appear to be a suitable landing zone on the north side of the hotel, which had a gentle upslope, but the surface was uncertain. By this time, Krutoff had reported back to Fliegerkorps XI. Although he had been prevented from reaching the hotel by a carabinieri guard post, Krutoff observed an excessive amount of security around Assergi, which tended to confirm

8 A nickname in intelligence work for discovering the vital piece of information that confirms or denies a priority intelligence requirement.
9 The Italian Comando Supremo had passed the location to the Allies as part of the armistice negotiations still under way.

that Mussolini was located on or near the Gran Sasso. As the indicators pointing to the Hotel Campo Imperatore added up, Student began contemplating a new rescue plan, but the Italian political situation abruptly changed and temporarily put the rescue of Mussolini on hold.

The Italian armistice

While Student and Skorzeny were searching for Mussolini, Badoglio and his band of conspirators had spent five fruitless weeks negotiating covertly with the Allies in Portugal. Badoglio was unhappy with the way that negotiations were going; rather than welcoming an Italian armistice, Allied negotiators maintained their tough demands for an "unconditional surrender," which seemed excessive to the Italians. Furthermore, Badoglio wanted the Americans to land an airborne division near Rome right after the announcement of an armistice, but this was deemed impractical. Instead, Badoglio began to have second thoughts about the armistice, which frustrated the Allies. With time running out before the Allied invasion at Salerno, General Eisenhower decided to announce the Italian armistice whether or not the Italians agreed. At 1630 hours on September 8, Allied radio networks began broadcasting the terms of the Italian surrender. Italy's deception was now revealed.

Although Kesselring's forces were outnumbered by more than two to one in the vicinity of Rome, he immediately began moving the 3.Panzergrenadier-Division from the north and the 2.Fallschirmjäger-Division from the south to converge upon the capital. Initially, the Germans were able to disarm some Italian units without lethal force, but the first clashes occurred around the Magliana Bridge around 2200 hours. German paratroopers fought two battalions of the Grenadiers of Sardinia, carabinieri, and troops from the Polizia dell'Africa Italiana (PAI), a colonial police unit that was formed for service in North Africa but which also played a role in regime security. Italian resistance stiffened when tanks and armored cars from the Ariete Armored Division arrived. But once the conspirators realized that they were actually going to have to fight the Wehrmacht, they chose to abandon their capital, their troops, and any lingering fragments of dignity, and fled for their lives. At 0510 hours on September 9, the king and queen, accompanied by Badoglio, General Ambrosio and

Italian soldiers surrendering to paratroopers from 2.Fallschirmjäger-Division on September 9–10, 1943. The concurrent need to disarm Italian troops after the announcement of the Badoglio armistice served as a major distraction to the forces involved in planning the raid to rescue Mussolini. (Bundesarchiv, Bild 101I-568-1539-19, Fotograf: Benschel)

Italian police and soldiers surrendering to Fallschirmjäger in Rome, September 10, 1943. However, not all Italians gave up without a fight and the units involved in the raid suffered significant casualties as a result. (Bundesarchiv, Bild 101I-568-1537-11, Fotograf: Benschel)

other senior officers, fled Rome eastward using the one road not yet secured by the Germans. Although there were almost 60,000 Italian troops around Rome, they were left virtually leaderless and without orders. Nor did the fleeing conspirators consider taking Mussolini south with them to Brindisi, where they would establish a new pro-Allied regime.

On the morning of September 9, Kesselring moved forcefully to crush all resistance in Rome and ordered German troops to disarm every Italian unit. In a surprise stroke, Student ordered the II/FJR 6 to conduct a parachute assault at Monterotondo, northeast of Rome, in the hope of capturing the Comando Supremo headquarters located in Orsini Castle. However, the Italians put up unexpectedly fierce resistance, beginning with heavy flak fire that badly scattered the airborne drop. Once on the ground, the disorganized German Fallschirmjäger companies found that they were up against two Italian infantry battalions, an artillery battery, a carabinieri detachment and even armed civilians. The Germans eventually fought their way to the castle against heavy resistance, but the senior Italian generals had already fled with the king. This failed operation cost II/FJR 6 135 casualties against 156 Italian casualties.

South of Rome, the I/FJR 7 under Major Harald Mors also encountered fierce resistance when it attempted to disarm the Italian Piacenza Semi-Motorized Division at Albano; 12 paratroopers were killed, including a platoon leader from the 1 Kompanie. Skorzeny's SS detachment was used in an auxiliary role and some of his NCOs were used as messengers. Further complicating Kesselring's situation, reports began arriving that morning about a major Allied landing at Salerno, so the Germans would have their hands full dealing with both Italians and the Allies. When the Italian fleet decided to sail to Malta to surrender, the Luftwaffe sank the battleship *Roma*, killing 1,350 Italian sailors. The gloves were off in German–Italian relations.

Italian armed resistance faded quickly though once Kesselring threatened to firebomb Rome and it became apparent that the Allied reinforcements were not going to arrive at any moment. Generale di Divisione Calvi di Bergolo negotiated a surrender of the Italian forces around Rome, which brought a halt to most of the fighting by 1600 hours on September 10. However, the bulk of the 2.Fallschirmjäger-Division was tied up for days in disarming Italians and restoring order in Rome. All told, the Germans suffered 619 casualties in the fighting around Rome and the Italians suffered 1,295 casualties.

PLANNING OPERATION *OAK*

With Rome secured by the morning of September 11, Student returned to the question of finding Mussolini. Now that the Allies were ashore in Salerno and the Italians were officially enemies, Student suddenly refocused on Mussolini. He realized that it was only a matter of time until the former Duce was either executed or handed over to the Allies. Although the best available information pointed to Gran Sasso, it was fragmentary at best. Nevertheless, Student decided to act as soon as possible and around 1500 hours ordered Major Harald Mors to begin planning a rescue mission to Gran Sasso to be conducted at 0730 hours on September 12 – only 16 ½ hours later. Student informed Mors that he could use the bulk of his I/FJR 7 for the raid, minus the 4 Kompanie, which was retained in Rome on security duties. Mors spent about an hour consulting with Langguth and Student's Ia (Operations officer), Major Arnold von Roon. Mors was unhappy about the skimpy intelligence about the Gran Sasso, but pressed on.

Once the "where" and "when" were nailed down, the next question in mission planning was "how." The three basic means to reach the Gran Sasso were either by parachute, by glider, or by ground assault. Although Student considered a parachute landing, Mors quickly ruled this method out owing to the possibility that it could be badly scattered atop a windy mountain plateau, resulting in heavy German casualties and a delay in reaching Mussolini. A ground assault against the hotel itself was also deemed impractical, since there were no roads leading to the mountaintop and an infantry assault up the mountainside would probably be detected early enough to give Mussolini's guards sufficient time to evacuate him. The bulk of the Italian 24th Infantry Division Pinerolo was located only 12km away in L'Aquila, which could pose a threat to the raiding force if surprise was lost or if they dallied too long at Gran Sasso. Since transport planes could not land atop the Gran Sasso, Mors realized that the only practical means to secure an exit route for the raiding force was for part of his force to mount a ground assault against the lower cable-car station in Assergi. The imagery collected by Skorzeny and Langguth was very poor, but it did suggest a small, flat landing area on the west side of the Hotel Campo Imperatore. While no one had ever done a glider assault at this altitude on this type of terrain, it did seem to offer the only fairly reliable means of getting a raiding force close enough to the hotel to overcome the guards before they had a chance to react. If the guards were given time to react, there would likely be significant German casualties and Mussolini would be either dead or gone, resulting in mission failure. Thus surprise was regarded as the key to mission success.

Student ordered 12 DFS-230 gliders from the 12th Staffel/Luftlande Geschwader 1[10] brought in to Pratica di Mare airfield as soon as possible, in order to provide lift for a company-size force to mount the main attack against the hotel. Mors selected Oberleutnant Georg Freiherr von Berlepsch's 1 Kompanie, reinforced with an additional platoon from the 4 Kompanie, to conduct the glider assault. Since each glider could carry nine troops, plus the pilot, Berlepsch would have a total of 120 men for his part of the raiding force. Student ensured that Berlepsch's 1 Kompanie received about a dozen of the new 7.92mm Fallschirmjäger gewehr 42 (FG-42-1) assault rifles, which was expected to give the Fallschirmjäger a significant firepower advantage in the assault.

Although Student and Mors were unsure about the exact size of the landing zone next to the hotel, it was clearly smaller than the one used atop Fort Eben Emael in

SEPTEMBER 9–10 1943

Kesselring crushes resistance in Rome

---

10 Also known as Sonderstaffel Heidenreich, since it was under the command of Oberleutnant Heidenreich.

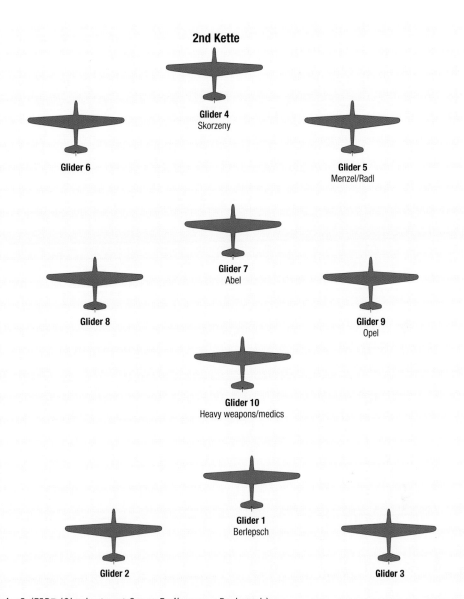

2nd Kette

Glider 4
Skorzeny

Glider 6

Glider 5
Menzel/Radl

Glider 7
Abel

Glider 8

Glider 9
Opel

Glider 10
Heavy weapons/medics

Glider 1
Berlepsch

Glider 2

Glider 3

1. Kompanie, I./FJR7 (Oberleutnant Georg Freiherr von Berlepsch)
    1st Platoon (Leutnant Joswig)
    2nd Platoon (Feldwebel Eugen Abel)
    3rd Platoon (Leutnant Gradler)

4. Kompanie, I./FJR7
    2nd Platoon (Leutnant Gerhard Opel)

SS-Jäger-Bataillon 502 (SS-Haupsturmführer Otto Skorzeny)
    Detachment, 1. Kompanie (SS-Obersturmführer Ulrich Menzel)

Tactical Assignments:
Kette 1 (Berlepsch): Main assault force. Seize Hotel.
Kette 2 & Glider 10: (Skorzeny): Support Force. Provide heavy weapons fire if needed and medical support.
Kette 3: (Abel/Opel): Reinforce assault force. One platoon will seize the upper cable car station.

MAJOR OTTO HARALD MORS AND THE FALLSCHIRMJÄGER-LEHR BATAILLON

After the heavy losses on Crete in May 1941, the Luftwaffe decided to form a special airborne unit that could test new equipment and methods of conducting vertical assaults. A Fallschirmjäger-Lehr Bataillon was formed in August 1941, using veterans who had served on Crete. In 1942, a second Lehr battalion was formed. Unfortunately, both battalions were sent to North Africa where they were lost in Tunisia in May 1943. A third Lehr unit, only at company-strength, was sent to join the newly forming 2.Fallschirmjäger-Division in France in May 1943, where it was redesignated as the I/FJR 7. However, due to its continued role as an experimental unit, the battalion was often still referred to as the Fallschirmjäger-Lehr Bataillon. In the summer of 1943, the battalion conducted extensive airborne and glider training, including use of DFS-230 gliders.

Following Mussolini's overthrow, the battalion was flown from France to Pratica di Mare airbase south of Rome, then moved to an encampment near Kesselring's headquarters in Frascati. Impressed by the battalion's skill at conducting mass jumps and specialized glider landings in France, Student designated the battalion as his quick-reaction unit in the event Mussolini was found. The unit was billeted in some olive groves near Frascati, which made it easy for Student to issue it a warning order as soon as Mussolini's location was discovered. Major Otto Harald Mors temporarily took over the battalion on August 1 since the normal commander was ill, but he was no stranger to the airborne. Mors had been born in Alexandria, Egypt in 1910 and his family returned to the Fatherland at the start of World War II. In 1935 he joined the Luftwaffe. Three years later Mors was overheard making anti-Hitler remarks and the Gestapo started a file on him. Once the war began, he served

on Student's staff in Crete in 1941 and then went to fight in the Soviet Union in 1942. By 1943 Mors was a professional airborne officer with a wealth of staff and combat experience that provided him with the means to plan and execute a mission like Operation *Oak*. The Fallschirmjäger-Lehr Bataillon was virtually the only unit then available that could have planned and successfully conducted a glider assault atop a mountain; without the skill and experience of leaders such as Major Mors and Oberleutnant von Berlepsch, the rescue of Mussolini would not have been possible.

Mors was captured in the Ruhr Pocket in 1945 but, due to his Gestapo file and perceived anti-Nazi leanings, the Americans released him after only a brief period in captivity. In 1956, he joined the newly formed Bundeswehr and eventually rose to the rank of Oberst before retiring in 1969. Although critical of Skorzeny in private, Mors made no real effort to contest the SS version of the Gran Sasso raid and for this reason, it was not until the 50th anniversary reunion at Campo Imperatore in 1993 that the accepted version began to unravel. There is no doubt that the credit and awards given to Skorzeny and his "SS Commandos" rankled Mors and his Fallschirmjäger comrades who knew the truth about the raid, but Mors' behavior appears somewhat hypocritical. On the one hand he disparaged the regime, but on the other he complained when that same regime did not sufficiently recognize and reward his professional skill. Instead, the regime chose to hype the role of the man who best exemplified Nazi virtues – Otto Skorzeny. Mors did not get the Ritterkreuz or public recognition for the raid, but he was able to live in his homeland and serve honorably in the postwar military, while Skorzeny was on the run and forced to spend the rest of his life in exile in Spain.

the 1940 glider assault. Heidenreich's DFS-230 gliders were a mix of the B- and newer C-models (which had braking rockets) and were capable of landing in as short a distance as 20 meters, although the slope of the ground could make this problematic.

Information about the Italian force guarding Mussolini was virtually non-existent, but Langguth estimated that about 100 Italian carabinieri were at the hotel itself and perhaps another 100 around the lower cable station. Based upon their experiences in Rome, the Fallschirmjäger expected the carabinieri to put up significant resistance and the assault troops would be highly vulnerable in the opening moments of the raid. Langguth was able to provide some information on the weather around the Gran

Sasso from Luftwaffe sources, which indicated low clouds and high winds around the mountaintops that could seriously disrupt the glider landings. The best time for a glider landing would be early morning, before the sun had a chance to heat the mountain air and cause further turbulence from rising currents.

As for the ground phase of the operation, Mors intended to mount his second and third companies on Fiat trucks captured from the Italian Piacenza Division two days earlier and use them to seize the lower cable-car station in Assergi. All told, Mors had about 260 troops and 20 vehicles in his column. Since Assergi was more than 100km from the Pratica di Mare airfield, Mors would have to depart with the ground force only 12 hours after receiving his mission order from Student.

A lower-priority component of the operation also concerned the rescue of Mussolini's wife and children from the castle-like Rocca delle Caminate, where they had been imprisoned since July. Kappler's operatives had sought to find where Mussolini's family was being held in the hope of getting further leads on the Duce's location. Since this task didn't require any special-operations expertise, Student gladly handed it to Skorzeny, who decided to send an 18-man team under Unterstumführer Hans Mändel to rescue Mussolini's family members to coincide with the main raid on Gran Sasso. Mändel was instructed to move in and liberate Mussolini's family at 1400 hours, in order not to provide any advance warning to the Italians that the Germans were mounting an operation to rescue Mussolini. However, Student's gesture was a mistake, since it now gave Skorzeny's men involvement in the raid phase of the operation, not just the search phase.

As the night went on, huddled over the skimpy maps and photos of Gran Sasso and planning load lists, Mors and Student became increasingly concerned about the extraction plan. After rescuing Mussolini, Mors intended to bring the Duce down to Assergi by cable car but, in case that was damaged in the fighting, Student provided two Fi-156 Fiesler Storch light planes that could possibly land and take off from atop the landing zone next to the hotel. Since Italian partisans were already actively harassing German convoys, and troops from the nearby Pinerolo Division might have time to establish roadblocks to hinder the exfiltration of the raiding force, Student also designated two Fallschirmjäger companies to be

A DFS-230B glider deploying its braking parachute during training in Italy in the summer of 1943. By using its parachute, the glider could typically stop in as little as 20–30 meters. (Bundesarchiv, Bild 101I-568-1531-32, Fotograf: Dr Stocker)

DFS-230B

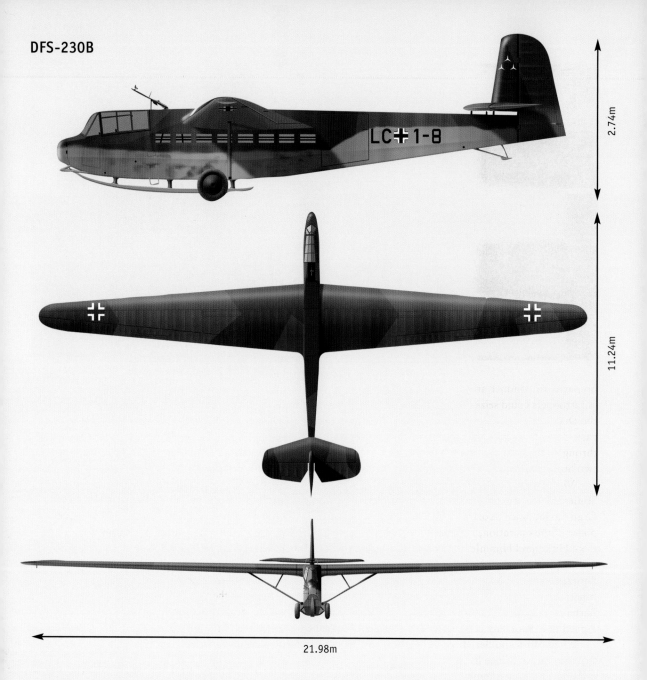

2.74m

11.24m

21.98m

DFS-230B	
Entered service	October 1939
Crew	1 Pilot
Passengers	9
Weight (empty)	860kg
Maximum payload	1,240kg
Maximum glide speed	290km/h
Normal tow speed	180km/h

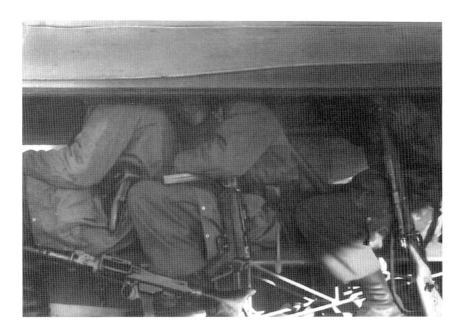

This photo shows the extremely cramped quarters inside a DFS-230 glider. Nine Fallschirmjäger sat one behind the other on a narrow, padded bench. Personal weapons could be kept close at hand, but equipment such as the MG-34 machine gun had to be stowed on the floor. (Bundesarchiv, Bild 101I-569-1179-25, Fotograf: Dr Stocker)

prepared to conduct an airborne drop on the airfield at L'Aquila. If needed, the paratroopers could seize the airfield long enough for transports to fly in and remove the Duce and the non-motorized part of the raiding force. Planning for the worst case, Mors also decided that his motorized column might have to fight its way through barricades either going in or on the way out and asked Student to provide two StuG-III assault guns for armored support.

While Mors was preoccupied with the final planning, Skorzeny approached Student and asked that some of his troops should be included in the raid against Gran Sasso. Since Skorzeny already figured in the low-key Rocca delle Caminate phase of the operation, he had his foot in the door and he invoked the instructions from Hitler and Himmler to suggest that his role should not be limited only to the search phase. For reasons that are unclear, Student buckled and agreed to allow Skorzeny and 17 of his men to participate in the glider assault, although their function was to act as bodyguards for the Duce during the extraction, freeing Berlepsch's Fallschirmjäger to fight Italians, if needed. Student also foolishly agreed that Skorzeny could escort Mussolini back to Germany after the rescue.

When Mors and Berlepsch heard about the inclusion of Skorzeny's detachment they were upset, since it meant leaving 18 of their own experienced troops behind in favor of taking a bunch of SD-types along as "baggage," but they nevertheless complied. Student told Mors, "He [Skorzeny] has no competence; he is participating as an observer . . ."[11] Approaching midnight, Mors had enough to worry about since it was clear that the gliders would not arrive at Pratica di Mare in time for an early morning assault and the ground column would not be in position in time. Student agreed to delay H-Hour to 1400 hours on September 12, but rejected Mors' request for a 24-hour delay since he was concerned that the Italians might get wind of the rescue and move Mussolini at any moment. At 0300 hours on September 12, Mors moved out of Frascati with the ground column toward Assergi.

SEPTEMBER 12 1943

0300 hours Mors' column moves out

---

11 Herman Götzel, *Generaloberst Kurt Student und seine Fallschirmjäger: die Erinnerungen des Generaloberst Kurt Student*, Podzun-Pallas-Verlag, Friedberg (1980)

One of the Hs-126 tow planes from Luftlande Geschwader 1 in Italy, summer 1943. These aircraft had difficulty reaching sufficient altitude while towing gliders to clear some of the tall Apennine peaks, which contributed to the bungled transit to the target on the day of the raid. (Bundesarchiv, Bild 101I-566-1492-17A, Fotograf: Dr Stocker)

Berlepsch organized the Gran Sasso raiding force into four groups, based upon the standard German glider tactic of operating in a three-glider *kette*. Mors provided several attachments from the battalion to Berlepsch, including a four-man signals detachment with Torn. Fu.d2 VHF/AM portable radios, a two-man medical section, a machine-gun section with two MG-42s, a mortar section with two 50cm le.GrW 36 light mortars, and a Panzerjäger team with one 2.8cm sPzB 41 tapered-bore anti-tank gun (139kg without ammunition). Although the inclusion of an anti-tank gun might seem odd, Berlepsch wanted a means to break into the hotel quickly in case the Italians had fortified the entrances; the sPzB 41 could fire both high-explosive and armor-piercing tungsten carbide rounds. Planning to fight outnumbered, Berlepsch wanted an edge in firepower.

Berlepsch would lead the first *kette*, with three gliders and 30 troops of the 1st Platoon, to begin the landing operation and conduct the initial assault on the hotel. His group had most of the FG-42 assault rifles (Berlepsch carried an MP-40 machine pistol), which they would use to gain firepower superiority over the guard force in the first few seconds of the raid. Skorzeny and his SS troops would be in the second *kette* and were primarily tasked with securing the landing zone and guarding any Italian prisoners. Once Mussolini was rescued, Skorzeny's men would provide security for him until extraction. The third *kette*, with Feldwebel Eugen Abel in charge of the 2nd Platoon, would capture the upper cable-car station, and the fourth *kette*, with Leutnant Gradler's 3rd Platoon, the heavy weapons, signal and medical troops, would help to secure the area around the hotel and provide support in case a protracted battle around the hotel occurred. Berlepsch wanted his first three gliders to land together nearly simultaneously, to provide the maximum assault force in the first moments of the raid, but after that individual gliders would be landing about one minute apart. Thus, it would take about 10 minutes to land the entire assault force.

Skorzeny, although not formally involved with the mission planning, continue to tinker with it behind Mors' back. Impulsive by nature, Skorzeny decided to include an Italian general in the operation, hoping to confuse or bluff their way past Mussolini's security detail. Upon Kappler's recommendation, Skorzeny sent Radl into Rome on the morning of September 12 to pick up Generale di brigata Fernando Soleti, a member of the PAI, whom the Gestapo had identified as having some knowledge of the security force guarding Mussolini on Gran Sasso. Kappler's sources noted that Soleti dispatched some of his PAI troops to the Gran Sasso on September 8, which further confirmed that this was the location where Mussolini was being held. Soleti had also played a minor role in the coup that overthrew Mussolini, but when confronted by the Gestapo he suddenly became cooperative and provided what information he could about the target (which was not incorporated into Major Mors' plan since he was already en route to Assergi). Skorzeny seized upon Soleti as a potential means of gaining entry into the hotel without shooting and ordered Radl to bring him to the Pratica di Mare airbase. Soleti was finally brought in around 1000 hours under the pretense of providing more information about

Inside the passenger compartment of a DFS-230 glider, looking forward. Note the separation between the passengers and the pilot, which invalidates much of Skorzeny's account of his role in steering Leutnant Meyer toward the landing zone. Once on the ground, the glider pilot would mount an MG-34 machine gun in the hatchway at the top. (Author's collection)

Mussolini's captors, but once he arrived he was placed under guard and told that he would participate in the rescue operation in an effort to spare bloodshed. Soleti had no desire to join in a glider assault but was given no choice. Another last-minute Skorzeny decision was to bump two more Fallschirmjäger to make room for a war correspondent and a photographer – it was becoming clearer by the minute that Skorzeny was more interested in the public relations side of the mission than any tactical details.

THE RAID

The ground assault

Although Frascati was only 93km from the village of Assergi, where the lower cable-car station up to the Gran Sasso was located, Major Mors elected to take a much longer and circuitous route with his motorized column. There had been recent fighting between Italian and German units near the more direct route through Tivoli, as well as reports of civilian unrest and partisan activity. Instead, Mors led his column southeast in a long detour toward Ferentino and then back to the northwest along the Liri Valley.

The column was led by a motorcycle scouting detachment, proceeding some distance ahead of the main body, which consisted of about 15 Fiat trucks loaded with Oberleutnant Karl Schulze's 3rd Company and the Battalion Stab Company. Major Mors rode in a command car toward the front of the main body. A platoon of Panzerjägers, a signal detachment, and the two assault guns[12] were in the rear of the column. The battalion's 2nd Company was currently broken up, with some troops attached to Schulze's company and others left behind at Frascati.

Mors' column encountered no resistance along the way, but it was spotted several times by Italian police, who relayed its location to other stations in the area. By late morning the *polizia* were aware that a German column was advancing toward the Abruzzi region, although its target was uncertain. Instead of a rapid blitz move to the target, Mors' column limped along in its captured Italian vehicles, which threatened to compromise operational security. Progress was very slow and it was not until 1300

Major Mors formed a motorcycle recon team to lead his column toward Assergi. These sidecar-equipped Zündapp machines were on loan from various support units in Fallschirmjäger Division 2. (Bundesarchiv, Bild 101I-567-1503D-27, Fotograf: Toni Schneiders)

12 Some accounts suggest that these were either Pz III or Pz IV medium tanks (possibly from the 26th Panzer Division) but photographs of the 2.Fallschirmjäger-Division in this period show it working with StuG III assault guns.

hours – ten hours after leaving Frascati – that the column reached the turn-off to Assergi near L'Aquila. Mors ordered Schulze to leave a blocking detachment (probably a platoon) at the intersection to warn of any interference by the Pinerolo Division and then the main body proceeded the last eight kilometers toward Assergi. Forty-five minutes later, Mors was close enough to the Gran Sasso to spot the Campo Imperatore Hotel with his binoculars. Realizing that X-Hour was still fifteen minutes away, Mors ordered the motorcycle-scout detachment to proceed cautiously into Assergi, since the cable-car station was on the northeast outskirts of the town, looking for any signs of resistance.

The carabinieri guarding the lower cable station had established several security checkpoints around the town to warn of intruders and they were alert when the Germans arrived. A forest guard named Pasqualino di Tocco, posted at a barricade south of Assergi, was the first to spot the German motorcyclists and when he attempted to warn the carabinieri in the village, the Fallschirmjäger shot and mortally wounded him with a burst of fire from their MP-40s. By the time the German scouts drove into Assergi, they were fired upon by several carabinieri located in buildings. Again, the Germans sprayed the likely hostile firing positions with automatic-weapons fire, inducing most of the carabinieri to break off the fight, but one carabinieri named Giovanni Natali was killed. Two other carabinieri were injured

SEPTEMBER 12 1943

0500 hours Glider assault troops assemble at Pratica di Mare

The advance on Gran Sasso

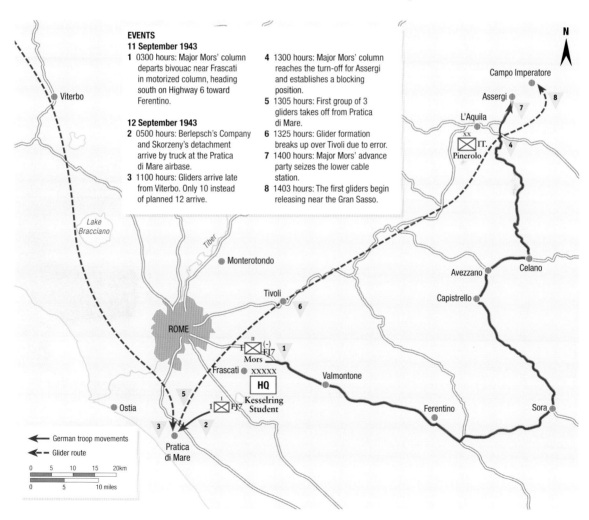

EVENTS

11 September 1943

1 0300 hours: Major Mors' column departs bivouac near Frascati in motorized column, heading south on Highway 6 toward Ferentino.

12 September 1943

2 0500 hours: Berlepsch's Company and Skorzeny's detachment arrive by truck at the Pratica di Mare airbase.

3 1100 hours: Gliders arrive late from Viterbo. Only 10 instead of planned 12 arrive.

4 1300 hours: Major Mors' column reaches the turn-off for Assergi and establishes a blocking position.

5 1305 hours: First group of 3 gliders takes off from Pratica di Mare.

6 1325 hours: Glider formation breaks up over Tivoli due to error.

7 1400 hours: Major Mors' advance party seizes the lower cable station.

8 1403 hours: The first gliders begin releasing near the Gran Sasso.

German troop movements

Glider route

0 5 10 15 20km

0 5 10 miles

One of the captured Italian vehicles used in Major Mors' dust-covered column. The approach march was too long and obvious, which provided some indication to the Italians that a German operation in the Abruzzi region was underway, but the men guarding Mussolini failed to take advantage of this early warning. (Bundesarchiv, Bild 101I-567-1503D-35, Fotograf: Toni Schneiders)

by a hand grenade thrown by the Germans. At this point, most of the carabinieri decided they were under attack by a far superior force and scattered. The scouting detachment drove on to the lower cable station and the few remaining Italians there quickly surrendered. Mors and the main body arrived shortly thereafter and found that the station was intact and that hostile resistance had been unexpectedly light. At 1417 hours the signal detachment with Mors received the signal "Mission accomplished" from the glider element. After securing the area around the lower station Mors, Oberleutnant Schulze and a few other Fallschirmjäger got in a cable car and began the ascent to the Gran Sasso.

Meanwhile, Untersturmführer Hans Mändel arrived with his detachment at the castle-like home of Mussolini in Rocca delle Caminate around X-Hour. The *polizia* agents guarding Rachele Mussolini and her two youngest children were not expecting a German raid and they quickly surrendered to Mändel and his men. He then bundled Mussolini's family into a car and whisked them to the airfield at Rimini, where they were put aboard a Luftwaffe aircraft and flown to Vienna.

Take-off from Pratica di Mare

The glider assault troops assembled at the Pratica di Mare airbase around 0500 hours on the morning of September 12, expecting the gliders to arrive at any time. While Berlepsch's Fallschirmjäger checked their weapons and equipment, Skorzeny's men – ignorant about glider operations – foolishly ate a large breakfast, including generous portions of rum. Skorzeny and Radl were almost totally absorbed for the entire morning with the General Soleti episode and took little interest in the flurry of last-minute details about the raid.

Unfortunately, the gliders were late in arriving. It was not until around 1100 hours that the gliders began arriving at Pratica di Mare (towed by Hs-126 aircraft) and it turned out then only ten, not 12, were brought in from Grosseto, north of Rome. In one of the mistakes that commonly plague a close-hold operation, the

transport unit had not been adequately briefed as to the requirements and timeline of Operation *Oak* and they had assumed that additional gliders could be brought in later in the day. There was no time to wait for more gliders to be brought in, so the plan was quickly adjusted to a ten-glider raid. Student arrived at the airfield around 0900 hours in order to give a final pep talk to both the Fallschirmjäger and Skorzeny's men.[13] It must not have been very uplifting, since Student warned the assembled troops that his staff estimated that up to 80 percent of the force might be lost due to glider crashes and enemy action. Since Student expected the Italians to fight, as they had at Monterotondo only three days earlier, Skorzeny's idea that the inclusion of an Italian general in the raiding force could avoid a firefight must have seemed naive. While the Hs-126 tow planes refueled, the troops were finally briefed on their objective and assigned specific sub-missions.

At 1210 hours, just as the troops were about to begin loading the gliders, an air-raid siren went off and loading operations ceased as everyone ran for shelters. Although the field was not bombed, the alarm caused another half-hour delay and it was not until 1300 hours that the raiding force was finally loaded. Inside each of the tightly packed DFS-230 gliders, which were a mix of the B- and C-models,[14] there was a pilot and, behind him, nine soldiers sitting one behind the other on a narrow bench. After the delay caused by the late glider arrival and the air-raid alarm, X-Hour was now barely an hour away and since it is unlikely that Mors was in radio contact with Pratica di Mare at this point, it would have been difficult to inform him of a postponement to X-Hour.

At 1305 hours, the first *kette* of three Hs-126 tow planes and DFS-230 gliders with Berlepsch's group took off and the rest followed at two-minute intervals.

General Student speaking to Skorzeny and his SS detachment at the airbase prior to the raid. Note that the SS men are wearing standard Wehrmacht Stahlhelm instead of airborne helmets, and Luftwaffe tropical uniforms instead of camouflage jump smocks. The SS men were also equipped with second-rate weapons and less infantry equipment compared to the Fallschirmjäger, indicating that they were not intended for an assault role. (Author's collection)

---

13 Skorzeny tried to introduce Soleti to Student in order to get some kind of recognition for his initiative in recruiting the Italian general, but Student was annoyed about the possibility that the mission's security was compromised by involving an Italian officer, particularly as Hitler had told them not to work with Kesselring's staff.

14 The B-Models had landing parachutes and the C-Model had braking rockets in the nose. Skorzeny's *kette* was equipped with B-Models.

SEPTEMBER 12
1943

1100 hours
Gliders arrive at
Pratica di Mare

SEPTEMBER 12
1943

1305 hours
Gilders take off

Langguth was in the lead Hs-126 to provide navigation to the target, since he was familiar with the terrain around Gran Sasso. The straight-line distance from Pratica di Mare to the Campo Imperatore was 126km. Once in the air, the groups headed northeast, passing south of Rome and then heading toward Tivoli. Shortly after leaving Pratica di Mare the flight began encountering strong winds, which slowed the climb rate of the underpowered tow planes and Langguth was concerned about the ability of the gliders to clear some 1,200-meter ridgelines near Tivoli. Before leaving Pratica di Mare, Langguth had apparently mentioned to some of the pilots that it might be necessary to execute a maneuver to get over the mountaintops, but not everyone got the word and this was not explicitly part of the plan. Around 1325 hours Langguth ordered his pilot to execute a lazy circle near Tivoli to gain more altitude before proceeding eastward. Although the three planes in this *kette* conducted the loop, the pilots in the following *kette*, who were about seven kilometers behind, became confused. Instead of circling, the following two groups simply proceeded on toward Gran Sasso, which put Skorzeny's group in the lead. Although Skorzeny later claimed that he ordered the pilot to proceed, Leutnant Meyer's after-action report reveals this as a fabrication. Furthermore, the cockpit inside the DFS-230 glider was separated from the passenger compartment by a divider, meaning that Skorzeny could not even see the pilot. Skorzeny and his men were simply passengers. Furthermore, many of Skorzeny's men were airsick, including General Soleti. Radl later reported that some of his men had vomited from airsickness inside their glider as well.

Inside glider no. 4, General Soleti sat immediately behind the pilot, Leutnant Meyer. Skorzeny was behind Soleti, followed by Untersturmführer Otto Schwerdt, Untersturmführer Robert Warger, Untersturmführer Andreas Friedrich, Rottenführer Himmel, Benz, Unterscharführer Hans Holzer, and Pföller. Glider no. 5 contained the rest of Skorzeny's men, including Obersturmführer Ulrich Menzel and Obersturmführer Karl Radl.

The tow planes approached Gran Sasso from the southwest, passing near L'Aquila, where they ran into strong gusts of wind and heavy cloud cover. Although the plan had called for an approach altitude of 3,200 meters, the tow planes decided to stay under the cloud cover, which was at 2,800 meters. Some of the Fallschirmjäger later claimed that they spotted Mors' ground column moving toward Assergi on the road below. Near Assergi, at 1403 hours, the gliders began to cut loose from the tow planes at an altitude of about 2300 meters and the glider pilots began a loop around the south side of the summit, maneuvering to approach the landing zone from the southeast. From the point of release, the gliders silently approached the target for about two minutes, and during this time they may have been observed by some of the guards around the hotel. After releasing the gliders, Langguth ordered his Hs-126 to circle the area to observe the raid, which may have also attracted attention. It was now 1403 hours, as the gliders of Skorzeny's *kette* turned toward the intended landing zone and began their final approach.

Last minute warning

Meanwhile it had been a restless night on the Gran Sasso. After hearing about the armistice on the evening of September 10/11 and that its terms called for him to be handed over to the Allies, Mussolini made a feeble attempt to commit suicide with a razor but was stopped by Tenente Faiola. Mussolini was convinced that he was going to be handed over to the Allies at any moment and put on trial, which drove him to despair. Thereafter, Faiola ensured that someone was with Mussolini at all times.

At least some Italians were aware that the Germans were up to something unusual that morning. Around 1130 hours Rodolfo Biancorosso, the police prefect of L'Aquila, called Inspector General Gueli at the Campo Imperatore Hotel and asked to meet him immediately at the lower cable-car station in Assergi. Gueli duly traveled down by cable car to meet Biancorosso, who informed him that a German attack on the Gran Sasso was imminent. In all likelihood, Biancorosso had been tipped off by outlying police stations that informed him about the progress of Mors' column, which was even then approaching L'Aquila. Gueli thanked him for the warning and returned to the upper station, where he increased the guard detachment there to about 40 men. However, he took no other special measures beyond telling Tenente Faiola to be alert.

This is the view from Assergi, looking toward the Gran Sasso. Clearly the terrain did not favor a company-size assault uphill and for this reason the Italians guarding Mussolini expected ample warning of any German raid. (Bundesarchiv, Bild 101I-567-1503-15, Fotograf: Bruno von Kayser)

GLIDER LANDINGS

1405 HOURS, SEPTEMBER 12, 1943

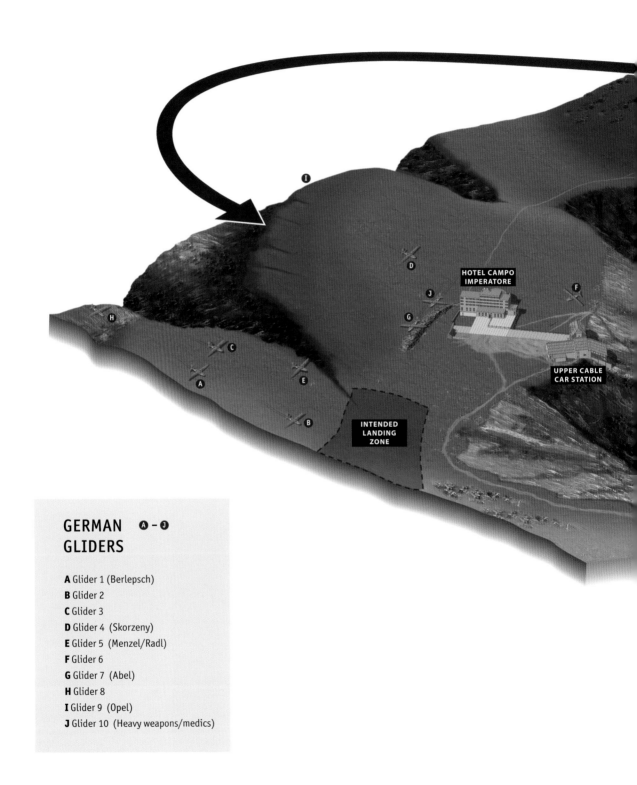

GERMAN GLIDERS Ⓐ – Ⓙ

A Glider 1 (Berlepsch)
B Glider 2
C Glider 3
D Glider 4 (Skorzeny)
E Glider 5 (Menzel/Radl)
F Glider 6
G Glider 7 (Abel)
H Glider 8
I Glider 9 (Opel)
J Glider 10 (Heavy weapons/medics)

KEY

Approach path

THE ITALIANS AT GRAN SASSO

The Italian security detachment guarding Mussolini at the Hotel Campo Imperatore was a mixed bag. Due to the nature of the conspiracy that overthrew Mussolini and uncertainty about loyalties, Badoglio did not want to hand the former Duce over to a single unit or commander. Instead, the security detachment was composed of both carabinieri military police and civil *polizia*. Inspector General Giuseppe Gueli was in charge of the 30-man police unit at Gran Sasso, which included a team of watchdogs, but their combat capability against regular troops was negligible. Indeed, Gueli later said that most of his policemen acted as if they were on a holiday. Gueli had made a name for himself in the Trieste area, suppressing socialist labor union activities and civil unrest, but he was essentially a thug with a badge. He joined the security detachment guarding Mussolini after Generale di brigata Polito was injured in a car accident in mid-August.

The 43-man carabinieri detachment was under the command of Tenente Alberto Faiola and his second-in-command, Tenente Osvaldo Antichi. Faiola had served under Badoglio in Ethiopia and had been personally entrusted with ensuring that Mussolini did not fall into German hands. Badoglio briefed Faiola on August 9 and spelled out that Mussolini was not to leave his place of imprisonment alive. The carabinieri were armed with two 6.5mm Breda M1930 light machine guns, 7.35mm carbines, and about 30 hand grenades.

After the outbreak of fighting between the Germans and Italians in Rome, Gueli asked for reinforcements and he received another 40–50 troops from various sources, including some PAI troops who escaped from Rome. The PAI troops brought four 9mm Beretta M1938 sub-machine guns with them. Faiola positioned the two Breda light machine guns outside the main entrance, which was barricaded inside with furniture from the hotel. In addition, the lower-level windows of the hotel were boarded up. However, most of the ammunition was stored in a room on the third floor. Gueli ordered that the police dogs be chained to protect "dead spaces" around the hotel, which meant they were positioned around the back side. On the day of the attack, about two-thirds of the 120-man security force was in or near the hotel, while about one-third were guarding the upper cable-car station.

Many of the troops were apparently inside and asleep, as was Gueli, when the raid began. Only about ten guards were posted on perimeter security around the building and apparently none were on the rooftop (which would have been an excellent position for a sniper). None of the guards had been adequately briefed on how to respond to an enemy attack.

Before the armistice had been announced, Badoglio instructed Faiola that he should execute Mussolini in the event of a German rescue attempt. However, once the Badoglio regime was on the run for their lives from Rome, Gueli became less inclined to follow its instructions and became more concerned about saving his own neck. He discussed the possibility of a German attack with Faiola and recommended that the guard force should not resist a major attack. Gueli was aware from his continued contact with police chief Carmine Senise in Rome that Hitler had ordered the execution of any Italian officer who resisted the Germans and he believed that saving Mussolini from execution might put him in a good light with the Germans. When the raid occurred, Gueli was committed to surrender but Faiola was undecided. It is clear that the Italians at Gran Sasso were aware that a German attack was possible, but they were not too imaginative in setting up their defenses and did not expect a glider or airborne assault.

The exact interaction between the Italians and the Germans in the opening moments of the raid is not clear, and the existing accounts are contradictory. It is clear that the Italians did not fire a shot and that at least some were allowed to retain their weapons after the hotel was occupied. Not only did the Italians help to clear the runway for Gerlach's plane, but they helped to bring in the wounded from glider no. 8. There was also a certain amount of drinking going on – off camera – between Italians and Germans. Indeed, it does not appear that the Italians actually surrendered so much as opted to "switch sides." Afterwards Gueli, Faiola and a number of carabinieri rallied to Mussolini's cause and followed him to the RSI in Salo after his rescue. Having been abandoned by the fleeing Badoglio regime, the guard force at Gran Sasso apparently decided that "when you can't beat 'em, join 'em."

The view from the cable car looking toward the lower station near Assergi. Major Mors' group succeeded in seizing the cable-car station intact, which greatly facilitated the exfiltration of the glider assault force. The ride from top to bottom typically took ten minutes. (Bundesarchiv, Bild 101I-567-1503C-26, Fotograf: Toni Schneiders)

Around 1330 hours, Gueli received another phone call from Biancorosso that relayed a message from police chief Carmine Senise in Rome that told him to use his own judgment in the event of a German attack, but suggested that an attack would not occur until the next morning. Gueli told Faiola to get some of the carabinieri to gather the mules that had been held in readiness in case they needed to bring Mussolini down the back side of the mountain. Expecting the Germans to occupy Assergi and the lower cable-car station, Gueli wanted to have an optional escape route ready just in case. If need be, they could move Mussolini that night under cover of darkness. Then, after giving these orders, Gueli retired to his room on the third floor for a siesta.

Landing at Campo Imperatore

While he was at Pratica di Mare airfield that morning, Student had emphasized that no gliders were to conduct crash landings, since experience on Crete had revealed that this often resulted in multiple injuries inside the glider. Even under the best landing conditions, Student expected that up to 80 percent of the gliders might suffer

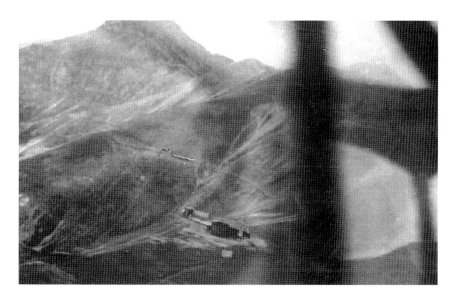

The Hotel Campo Imperatore seen from glider no. 6, which was the third to land. Skorzeny's glider is visible just to the right of the hotel, indicating that for several moments he and his team were the only Germans on the Gran Sasso. (Bundesarchiv, Bild 183-H27777, Fotograf: Bruno von Kayser)

Fallschirmjäger pour out of a glider during the filmed re-enactment of the raid, which Student orchestrated two weeks later. The man jumping out of the cockpit is armed with an FG-42 assault rifle and is wearing a bandolier for flare cartridges. (Author's Collection)

damage in trying to land atop the Gran Sasso and he warned the pilots against increasing the odds of casualties. Furthermore, the best chance for mission success was if the lead *kette* landed close together and nearly simultaneously, which was only possible with a controlled glide landing. However, the unfortunate misunderstanding near Tivoli had already scrambled the original plan and the actual landing was to be more ad hoc than intended.

Leutnant Meyer, piloting the lead glider with Skorzeny aboard, later reported that:

We continued to slowly gain altitude on an easterly course and soon saw the enormous Gran Sasso d'Italia, which was partly covered by clouds. Already three quarters of the flying time had gone by. A quick look at the map and the aerial photo confirmed the location. The black dot in the saddle-cut had to be the Campo Imperatore.

The Hotel Campo Imperatore, seen from Skorzeny's glider. The earth berm around the rear of the hotel prevented Skorzeny from getting a good look at the lower level and obscured the fact that there were no entrances on this side. The upper window shutters were open due to the heat – many of the Italian guards were on this level enjoying a siesta. (Bundesarchiv, Bild 101I-567-1503A-05, Fotograf: Toni Schneiders)

I pulled the release device with my left hand and saw the towrope disappear below, while the nose of the glider dropped toward the objective. The statements Skorzeny [later] made about giving me landing instructions were made up; it would be absurd for a passenger to give instructions to the commander of a glider echelon and besides, Skorzeny sat in a position in the glider from which he couldn't see the landing area.

The black dot on the mountain came up quickly. Despite extending the air brakes, the strong updrafts from the mountaintop pushed against the aircraft and it was difficult to keep on the glide path toward the target. Tensely, I tried to spot any hostile movement. First everything was calm and it looked as if the nest would be empty. It was only when we were about 150 meters from the hotel that suddenly, like ants, many people began to emerge from the exit. Already I could see details. The soldiers did not show a hostile attitude. They had rifles and submachine guns, but all just stopped and stared, obviously surprised by the unknown aircraft.

However, I could also see that the intended landing zone – in contrast to the aerial photograph [taken before the raid] – had steep slopes that dropped off into an abyss. Looking left and right, I could see that I was far ahead of the remaining gliders in my kette.

Therefore, I seized upon a quick resolution. I put the glider into a steep left circle, which pressed the passengers hard. I deployed the braking parachute as we approached the windy slope, heading straight toward the hotel. A jolt went through the glider when it first hit the hard, stony ground, tearing up the barbed wire wrapped under the skid like string. When the glider stopped, it stood only 40 meters away from the hotel.[15]

Meyer's glider came to rest in an open area on the east side of the hotel. It was now 1405 hours. Several Italian *polizia* stationed near the entrance had seen the

The upper cable-car station, photographed after the completion of the raid. The 1.5-meter-tall raised forecourt that Skorzeny had so much trouble climbing is in the foreground. Note that on the left, a Fallschirmjäger is standing on a small raised platform that provides an easy means of scaling the wall – apparently Skorzeny was not observant enough to notice this. (Bundesarchiv, Bild 101I-567-1503B-06, Fotograf: Toni Schneiders)

SEPTEMBER 12 1943

1403 hours Gliders cut loose

---

15 Oberleutnant Johannes Heidenreich, *Gefechtsbericht über den Einsatz der Sonderstaffel Heidenreich am 12.9.43.*

glider's approach at the last moment and one ran toward that end of the hotel to see where it had landed. Inside Meyer's glider, the SS men and Generale Soleti were badly knocked about by the crash landing. SS-Untersturmführers Schwerdt and Warger were the closest to the exit hatch; they opened it and fell out clumsily to the ground. Skorzeny, who was sitting forward of the exit, could only move slowly toward the hatch. General Soleti, who had wanted no part of this glider ride, followed Skorzeny. Stunned by the sudden impact with the ground and still shaky from airsickness, most of Skorzeny's men lingered around the fallen glider, uncertain what to do next since they had not been tasked with securing the hotel but now they were here first. The only one who knew what to do was Meyer, who began setting up the MG-34 machine gun on the mount above the cockpit, in accordance with standard Fallschirmjäger doctrine.

Once out of the glider, Skorzeny impulsively ran uphill toward the hotel, in plain view of a nearby *polizia* guard who began shouting a warning.[16] However, Skorzeny was in such a rush that he left his machine pistol behind in the glider and neglected to give his men any kind of orders. Ignoring the shouting guard, Skorzeny reached the rear of the hotel and cautiously opened the first door that he found. Inside, a single Italian soldier was working at a telephone switchboard.[17] Skorzeny was befuddled for a moment, expecting to find an entrance into the main part of the hotel but instead he was now standing in a poorly lit, dead-end room that only had a single entrance. Realizing his mistake, Skorzeny ran out of the room just as Schwerdt was entering it and together they moved along the rear side of the hotel, looking for a point of entry. By this time, two of the SS NCOs, armed with MP28 machine pistols, had recovered their wits and were finally following in the wake of Skorzeny and Schwerdt. Since the first-floor windows were all boarded up, the SS men could not see into the building and they were surprised by the lack of entry points. It is also possible that Skorzeny and his men ran into Gueli's guard dogs, which were chained on the back side of the hotel, causing further delay.

As Skorzeny moved toward the west side of the hotel, SS-Obersturmführer Ulrich Menzel's glider no. 5 crash-landed about 100 meters in front of the hotel. This was also a very rough landing and Menzel broke his ankle just after exiting his glider. Radl slowly got the men out of the glider, but they were badly shaken up and also uncertain what to do next. Indeed, the SS men were pretty useless in the opening moments of the glider assault, due to a combination of lack of training for this role and airsickness. Inside the hotel, Tenente Faiola had been alerted to the glider landings by the shouting *polizia* and, after telling several men to secure the entrance, he ran upstairs to the third floor to ask Gueli for instructions.

Skorzeny reached the west end of the hotel and was confronted with a 1.5-meter raised platform that he was unable to climb over. Unlike British commandos, Skorzeny's men did not have any obstacle-course training and he was momentarily stopped in his tracks by a simple wall. He failed to notice that there was an easy means of scaling the platform just 30 meters to his left. Stymied, Skorzeny fumbled about for a couple of minutes unable to get over the raised platform. Finally, Rottenführer Himmel caught up with him and Schwerdt and Skorzeny ordered Himmel to bend over so they could use his back as a platform to scale the wall.

---

16 Skorzeny may not have realized that the bulk of the raiding force had yet to arrive. In the plan, he did not expect to arrive until mid-raid and his impulsive rush may have been driven by a desire to "get in the action" before it was all over.

17 Skorzeny claims that he smashed the radio with the butt of his sub-machine gun, but photographs from Gran Sasso indicate that he was armed only with a Walther PPK pistol. Thus, he probably did not use force against this Italian.

At least five minutes had elapsed since Skorzeny's glider had first landed and he still had not made it to the entrance of the hotel.

While Skorzeny was trying to get over his obstacle, glider no. 6 landed between the hotel and the upper cable-car station. This glider nearly slid off into the abyss, but its troops emerged intact and move to secure the cable-car station. However, since both war correspondents were on that glider, this team had only seven assault troops aboard. Glider no. 7 with Feldwebel Eugen Abel's 2nd Platoon had also just landed against the earth berm on the east side of the hotel, closer than Skorzeny's glider. Meanwhile, the Italians were beginning to react to the first warning shouts and the guards stationed at the front entrance ran toward the east side of the hotel, where General Soleti and several Germans were still milling around Skorzeny's glider. Soleti was beginning to come alive, shouting and gesturing in a wild manner, which probably confused the guards. Tenente Faiola reached Gueli's room and woke the police inspector, who was asleep in the nude and was now caught literally with his pants down. Faiola asked Gueli, who stood before him naked and dumbfounded, "What do we do? Do we shoot Mussolini or evacuate him?" However, Gueli was still waking up and was slow to respond. While Faiola was on the third floor, the entrance was left virtually unguarded. Many of the Italian guards resting inside the hotel chose to hide in their rooms, rather than respond to Faiola's order to stand-to.

Eight Fallschirmjäger debarking from Leutnant Gerhard Opel's glider no. 9. The troops are moving upslope toward the hotel. (Bundesarchiv, Bild 101I-567-1503B-15, Fotograf: Toni Schneiders)

Opel left one Fallschirmjäger to guard the glider as he led the rest of his team to the hotel. This glider apparently suffered damage to its starboard wing tip. (Bundesarchiv, Bild 101I-567-1503B-17, Fotograf: Toni Schneiders)

The hotel seen from Opel's glider no. 9. Skorzeny's no. 3 glider is on the upper far left, followed by glider nos. 7 and 10 next to the berm around the hotel. This photo gives a good indication of how the ground rapidly fell off only a short distance from the hotel. It is also evident that glider no. 9 broke its starboard wing on the rocky surface. (Bundesarchiv, Bild 101I-567-1503B-23, Fotograf: Toni Schneiders)

Still undressed, Gueli finally looked out the window and saw more German gliders landing a couple of hundred meters away. In the distance, a group of five heavily armed German paratroopers were visible moving toward the hotel, but otherwise there were few others yet in sight. Gueli panicked, and yelled, "Don't shoot! Don't shoot!" to his bewildered sentries below. Realizing that Gueli, standing there naked and screaming in panic, was unable to think rationally at the moment, Faiola roused Osvaldo Antichi, his second-in-command, from his room and together they ran back toward Mussolini's room. They reached Room 201 and found Mussolini looking out the window at the glider landings. Faiola yelled at him to get away from the window and told him that he had been ordered by Maresciallo Badoglio not to let his prisoner fall into German hands. Sensing that he was about to get a bullet in the neck, Mussolini began arguing with him and Faiola was not certain whether he should kill Mussolini or try to escape down the mountain with him while his guards held off the Germans. Mussolini told Faiola that if he was killed the Germans would execute the entire guard force. With that, Faiola hesitated.

Glider no. 7 landed against the berm on the east side of the hotel. Notice the raised platform on this side and the shuttered lower-level windows, both of which slowed down German access into the hotel. (Bundesarchiv, Bild 101I-567-1503B-05, Fotograf: Toni Schneiders)

To be or not to be...

Outside, Skorzeny was finally atop the raised forecourt and he moved cautiously toward the front entrance of the hotel. He suddenly realized that he was way out in front and armed only with a pistol, so he grew more cautious and waited for more Germans to arrive. Although some of Radl's men were moving toward the hotel and a few other Germans were moving about near the cable station, there was no real concentrated assault force at hand to accompany him into the hotel. It was just Skorzeny and Schwerdt, facing perhaps 100 Italian guards inside the hotel. Several armed carabinieri were still outside the hotel gawking at the German glider landings, but when they saw Germans approaching they ran back inside the hotel and began to erect a barricade of furniture in the entranceway. SS-Untersturmführer Warger moved around the earth berm on the east side and approached the façade of the hotel, pushing General Soleti along (possibly with a pistol to his ribs) and urging him to call upon the guards not to resist. Soleti was unconvincing as an authority figure since he appeared to be almost a prisoner, but his appearance did confuse the guards further.

Prior to landing, Skorzeny had told his own men not to open fire unless he fired his weapon first and now he approached the entrance to the building with his pistol still holstered. Two Breda light machine guns were mounted on bipods near the entrance but had been abandoned by the guards when they ran back inside the building. Skorzeny could not get a good look at how many carabinieri were actually waiting inside and his first attempt to push open the door failed due to a barricade made of tables from the nearby dining room. Unlike Berlepsch's assault group, which had hand grenades to deal with such obstacles, Skorzeny and his men were only lightly armed. Unable to get in the only ground-floor entrance, Skorzeny decided to try and bypass it. He later claimed that, glancing upward, he spotted Mussolini looking out of a second-floor window. Apparently Gueli began yelling out of the window at Soleti, which caused Mussolini to look out again. Tenente Faiola ordered Mussolini to get away from the window, but the Duce ignored him until he was forcibly pulled away. Satisfied that Mussolini was inside and now aware of where he was located, Skorzeny ordered two of his men, Unterscharführer Hans Holzer and Rottenführer Albert Benz, to climb up the front side of the building and try to reach Mussolini's room. The two men succeeded in climbing up on a small structure and got near Mussolini's window, but could not get in the building either. However, now that more German troops were approaching the hotel Skorzeny and Schwerdt decided to make another go at the entrance and this time the Italian guards did not resist.

Once the objective was secured, Berlepsch ordered his radio team to notify Major Mors immediately. The Torn. Fu.d2 VHF/AM radio had sufficient range to contact Mors' group, but contact with Student's headquarters at Frascati was sporadic, which influenced the choice of exfiltration. (Bundesarchiv, Bild 101I-567-1503B-03, Fotograf: Toni Schneiders)

STORMING THE HOTEL

1405–1415 HOURS, SEPTEMBER 12, 1943

KEY

– – – – – – – – – – – – – – →

Skorzeny's route

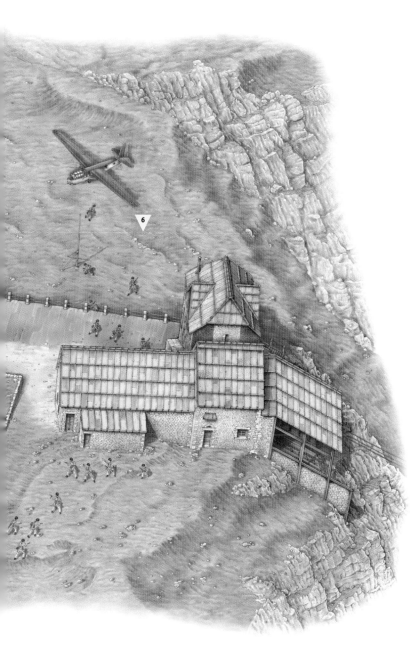

▼ EVENTS

1 Italian guards emerge from the entrance as the first German gliders appear overhead.

2 Skorzeny emerges from his glider, runs past an Italian guard toward the rear of the hotel and enters the radio room.

3 Failing to gain entrance to the hotel itself, Skorzeny runs around the back of the hotel. He may have run into Gueli's chained police dogs, causing delay. Then, he meets the raised forecourt, which he cannot climb alone.

4 After consulting with Gueli, Tenente Faiola runs to Mussolini's room.

5 Radl begins moving some of his SS men toward the front of the hotel.

6 Glider 6 lands between the hotel and the upper cable car station, and the Fallschirmjäger move to seize the station.

7 Glider 7 lands against the earth berm on the east side of the hotel and more Fallschirmjäger emerge. The Italian troops retreat back inside the hotel and barricade the entrance.

8 Buoyed by the appearance of more Fallschirmjäger and hearing no shooting, Warger and Soleti move toward the front of the hotel. Soleti calls upon the guards not to shoot, but few hear him.

9 Skorzeny finally makes it to the front of the hotel and sends two of his men to climb toward Mussolini's room.

10 Gueli sees more Germans nearing the front of the hotel and yells "Don't shoot!" to his men.

11 Skorzeny and Schwerdt force their way into the entrance and make their way to Room 201, where they disarm Faiola and Antichi, and liberate Mussolini.

12 Berlepsch's assault group reaches the front of the hotel and he orders his men to surround the building. He sends some troops to complete the occupation of the cable car station.

13 With the area secure and Italian resistance non-existent, Berlepsch orders his signal section to radio "Mission accomplished" to Major Mors.

This is a very peculiar photo that shows armed Italians freely walking around the area, inspecting glider no. 7. Skorzeny's glider is to the left. With the raid completed, both sides appear to be amazingly lackadaisical. (Bundesarchiv, Bild 101I-567-1503C-32, Fotograf: Toni Schneiders)

Although the narrow entrance was partially blocked with a barricade,[18] the Italian *polizia* were the first to lower their weapons. Most of the Italian guards either stood by impassively, unsure what to do, while others ran and hid in their rooms. There was no organized resistance.

Once inside the hotel, Skorzeny turned right and bolted up the short staircase and quickly reached the second floor. Skorzeny burst into Room 201 where Mussolini was being held and saw the Duce flanked by two Italian officers (Faiola and Antichi), neither of whom had a drawn weapon. At this point Skorzeny drew his pistol and beckoned the two Italian officers to stand against the wall. Schwerdt followed into the room a moment later and took charge of the two Italians, pushing them out in the hallway. Then, Skorzeny engaged in a theatrical speech to the surprised Mussolini. "Duce, the Führer sent me to free you!" he said, and then proceeded to lay it on thickly about his personal role in the search. After listening to Skorzeny, a tired Mussolini supposedly exclaimed, "I knew that my friend Adolf Hitler would not have abandoned me!" but quickly lapsed into small talk with Skorzeny and asked to be taken to his home at Rocca delle Caminate. About ten minutes had elapsed since Skorzeny's glider first touched down.

Outside the hotel, all ten gliders had landed by X+9 minutes (1412). Glider nos. 5, 6, and 7 had landed shortly after Skorzeny's and their troops had begun to round up some of the Italian guards, but there was no concerted drive on the hotel. At about X+5 (1408), the violent winds around the mountaintop destabilized Glider no. 8 as it was coming in for a landing and first pushed it away from the landing zone and then caused it to plummet sharply against the mountainside, breaking its right wing. Both the pilot (Feldwebel Ronsdorf) and several Fallschirmjäger were badly injured in this crash, but there were no fatalities. There were injuries from rough landings in other gliders as well, such as Feldwebel Bernd Bosshammer, who injured his knee. At around X+7 minutes (1410), the glider *kette* carrying Oberleutnant Berlepsch's assault element finally began to land in front of the hotel, close to the intended landing zone – it was the appearance of these three gliders that had caused Gueli to buckle. Berlepsch's three gliders executed a perfect landing and the Fallschirmjäger quickly disembarked and began running toward the hotel. Skorzeny apparently had not moved into the hotel until he saw Berlepsch's men approaching, aware that very few of his own men were behind him. The only shot fired during the entire glider part

---

18 Skorzeny's assertion that he and Schwerdt bulled their way through a crowd of carabinieri in the narrow entrance was a fabrication. If he pushed anything aside, it was furniture.

of the raid occurred when an inexperienced Fallschirmjäger accidentally fired his rifle into the air as he exited his glider.

When Berlepsch's assault group reached the entrance area, most of the Italian guards had run back inside and it was unclear whether they were fortifying the building or merely running away. Berlepsch saw no sign of Skorzeny (but Skorzeny had seen him), although he did see Holzer and Benz idiotically hanging on to the side of the building. Berlepsch played it by the book, first ordering his assault platoon to surround the hotel to prevent any escape out of other exits, then commanding one squad to remove the ad hoc barricade in the entranceway. He also ordered his machine-gun team to set up their MG-42 to cover the rear of the hotel in case there was any attempt by the Italians to escape. By this point, Berlepsch became aware that Skorzeny was inside the hotel on the second floor (the two SS men hanging outside the second-floor room were talking to him through the window) and that Mussolini was in German hands. Once the Germans began to tear down the barricade, some of the Italian carabinieri came out of the hotel and began to mingle with the approaching Fallschirmjäger. Oddly, Berlepsch did not order his men to disarm or even confine the former Italian guards, but merely chose to ignore them once it was clear that they would not resist.

Satisfied that the hotel was surrounded, Berlepsch ordered Leutnant Gerhard Opel, leading the 2nd Platoon attached from 4/FJR 1-7, to help the handful of men from glider no. 6 to secure the upper cable-car station. The carabinieri guarding the station were completely surprised and either handed their rifles over to the Germans or threw them off the cliff into the gorge below. Several Germans went below the station to secure the 50-meter-long underground tunnel connecting the station to the hotel. In minutes, it was over. After rounding up the 40-odd Italians in the cable-car station, a Fallschirmjäger got on the phone to the lower station and spoke to one of

Skorzeny and Berlepsch (to his right) have hurriedly joined the crowd around Mussolini. Three carabinieri – including one still clearly carrying his Beretta sub-machine gun – have jumped in front of an annoyed Skorzeny. This photo demonstrates that the Italian guard force was neither disarmed nor treated as prisoners. (Bundesarchiv, Bild 101I-567-1503C-16, Fotograf: Toni Schneiders)

The German officers have ordered their troops to stand back so they can get a photo with just them and Mussolini. Skorzeny seems pleased to be out in front with Mussolini, while Mors and Berlepsch are in the background. Gueli, finally dressed, is seeking a moment with his former prisoner to discuss his own fate. (Bundesarchiv, Bild 101I-567-1503A-03, Fotograf: Toni Schneiders)

SEPTEMBER 12
1943

1405 hours
First glider lands
at Campo
Imperatore

SEPTEMBER 12
1943

1412 hours
All gliders now
landed

Mors' men, informing them that the upper station had been taken: "*Hier Bergstation! Bergstation in unserer hand!*" Berlepsch also ordered his signal section to establish radio contact with Major Mors in the valley below and at 1417 hours they radioed "Mission accomplished!" From start to finish, the raid had taken only 12 minutes. Overhead, Langguth and Heidenreich continued to circle the Campo Imperatore in their HS-126 aircraft, trying to figure out what was going on below.

Inside Room 201, Skorzeny briefly left Schwerdt in charge of Mussolini and went down to the dining room on the first floor, just as some Fallschirmjäger were entering the hotel. To celebrate his success, Skorzeny began distributing bottles of wine from the dining room to both Italian carabinieri and his own SS men, which created something of a party atmosphere. When Skorzeny saw Berlepsch approaching, he returned to Room 201. He posted two of his SS men, Holzer (now inside the building) and Unterscharführer Robert Neitzel in the hallway outside the door.[19] It took a while to get Mussolini willing to move; he was tired from lack of sleep the night before and depressed by weeks of captivity. Initially he despondently muttered to Skorzeny, "Do what you like with me," but after a half-hour he pulled himself together a little. Skorzeny plied Mussolini with a steady stream of nonsense to boost his ego and assured him that he would be taken wherever he wanted (knowing full well that Hitler's orders were to bring him to Germany). After collecting up some of Mussolini's possessions in two suitcases, Skorzeny and Schwerdt led Mussolini out to the main entrance, with Faiola and Antichi in tow. Gueli had finally managed to get dressed and he arrived at the entrance as well. Before exiting the hotel, Mussolini turned to Antichi and reportedly stated, "I would have preferred to be freed by Italians." Skorzeny then led Mussolini out of the hotel around 1500 hours and ran straight into Berlepsch and Mors. It is not clear why Berlepsch himself had not gone up to Room 201 in the 40 minutes since the hotel had been secured, but he had probably focused more on running his company once he realized that Mussolini was in German hands. He did order his medics to bring the injured Fallschirmjäger into the hotel dining room, where they were tended to by the battalion surgeon, Dr Brunner. Both Berlepsch and Mors were infuriated with Skorzeny's apparent disregard for their tactical plan, but decided to save their criticism for another moment, when Mussolini was out of earshot.

---

19 In his postwar interrogation about the raid, Skorzeny claimed that SS-Oberscharführer Walther Gläsner and Sfaeller assisted in securing the room, but in his memoirs he claims it was Holzer. In his account, Holzer said the other SS man was Neitzel.

Exfiltration

After receiving news that the hotel had been secured, Major Mors quickly got in a cable car and ascended to the upper station, arriving at 1445 hours. Berlepsch met Mors near the station and gave him a quick run-down of the situation. After conveying that there were no fatalities or resistance, Mors shifted to discussing the exfiltration plan.

Prior to X-Hour, Student and Mors had discussed three possible means of bringing Mussolini back to Pratica di Mare airfield. The most secure plan envisaged bringing Mussolini down by cable car to the lower station and then driving him to the airfield at L'Aquila in Mors' vehicles. A flight of three He-111 bombers would then land at L'Aquila to pick up Mussolini and part of the rescue force. If necessary, a company of Fallschirmjäger would be flown in to secure the airfield ahead of time. However, Mors did not have radio contact with Student's headquarters at this point, so he could not call up the aircraft. Langguth was still circling overhead and could have been used as a relay, but for unknown reasons this was not considered. Skorzeny appeared eager to squash this exfiltration plan and suggested to Mors that the Italians had alerted the Allies about the raid and that an air attack could be expected at any moment, making it imperative to get Mussolini out immediately. Mors ignored him, but he did shift to Plan B.

As a back-up plan, Student had dispatched two Fi-156 Fiesler Storch light aircraft to support the operation and, if need be, pick up Mussolini from whatever landing spot could be secured. Troops from Mors' detachment fired a flare to indicate that the lower cable-car station was seized but when Oberfeldwebel Hundt tried to land his Storch on a seemingly flat piece of land near the station in Assergi he damaged his undercarriage on the uneven surface. It would take hours to make the Storch airworthy again. Around 1450 hours, Hauptmann Heinrich Gerlach (Student's personal pilot) brought his Storch around by the top of Campo Imperatore and succeeded in landing on a 30-meter stretch near the front of the hotel. Gerlach left the Storch in the care of several Fallschirmjäger and ran toward the hotel, where Mors and Berlepsch were discussing the situation. After hearing that Hundt's Storch

**SEPTEMBER 12
1943**

**1417 hours
Mission
accomplished
signal transmitted**

The Germans set their gliders on fire after the raid since they could not be recovered from the mountain. Some smaller components were salvaged and brought back. (Bundesarchiv, Bild 101I-567-1503D-05, Fotograf: Toni Schneiders)

Once Gerlach landed his Fiesler Storch on the plateau, a mixed group of SS, Fallschirmjäger, and Italians escorted Mussolini to the area that was being cleared for the take-off. While one Italian guard happily carries the Duce's suitcase, General Soleti, to Mussolini's left, appears to be walking in a trance. (Bundesarchiv, Bild 183-R99898, Fotograf: Bruno von Kayser).

was unavailable and that Mors was not in contact with Student, Gerlach agreed to fly Mussolini out in his Storch from the area near the hotel. Skorzeny ordered several of his men to begin clearing rocks away from the intended take-off path and 18 Italians cheerfully joined in.

When Mussolini emerged from the hotel, Skorzeny and Schwerdt were at his side. Mussolini wore a large black overcoat, and a hat covering much of his face, which was unshaven, and his clothes were worn and dirty after weeks of captivity. Numerous carabinieri crowded around Mussolini, excited by the moment and relieved that the war seemed over for them, while the German war correspondents Toni Schneiders and Bruno von Kayser began snapping photos. First Mors and Berlepsch, then Skorzeny and Schwerdt, posed with a reluctant Mussolini, who felt more like a trophy than a national leader. The German officers were surprised by Mussolini's disheveled appearance and listless attitude. Soleti, Gueli, and Faiola also

Hauptmann Gerlach returns to his Storch, followed by Schwerdt. The area in front of the plane has been quickly cleared of large rocks but it still lumpy. One of the glider pilots stands guard behind the tail plane with his MP-40. (Bundesarchiv, Bild 101I-567-1503C-03, Fotograf: Toni Schneiders)

The first poses outside the hotel after Mussolini's rescue. From left to right, one of Skorzeny's SS soldiers, Feldwebel Wächtler, Major Mors, Oberleutnant Karl Schulze, Mussolini, Soleti, Otto Schwerdt (who is apparently yelling to Skorzeny to get in the picture), Faiola, and Karl Radl. Five Italian soldiers are in the background. (Bundesarchiv, Bild 101I-567-1503C-14, Fotograf: Toni Schneiders)

managed to get in the pictures in order to talk to Mussolini about their fates.[20] Afterwards, Skorzeny took Gerlach aside and demanded that he accompany Mussolini in the Storch. Gerlach flatly refused, citing that Skorzeny would overload the aircraft and that the take-off run was dangerously short. Skorzeny was persistent and finally resorted to threats, and Gerlach relented.

Mussolini and Skorzeny walked toward the Fiesler Storch, surrounded by a mixed crowd of Germans and Italians. Photos indicate that a number of the Italian carabinieri were still armed. Gerlach climbed inside the cockpit, followed by Mussolini and then Skorzeny. Mussolini objected to this risky procedure but was ignored. In order to take off with the wind behind him, Gerlach revved the engine while several Fallschirmjäger held the wings, then began his take-off roll around 1515 hours. Normally the Storch needed about 80 meters to take off, but in the thin air at 2,000 meters and overloaded Gerlach needed all of the 200-meter stretch on the east side of the hotel. Using every bit of his aeronautical skill, Gerlach succeeded in getting the Storch airborne just before it reached the steep precipice, but even after getting off Campo Imperatore he had difficulty gaining altitude. Gerlach's left landing gear was damaged when it struck a rock during the take-off and the engine was malfunctioning. Mussolini was subjected to a nerve-wracking low-level flight, with Skorzeny crammed in behind him, until Gerlach gradually got a little altitude and headed westward. Gerlach finally reached the Pratica di Mare airfield with Mussolini and Skorzeny around 1615 hours, where they transferred to an He-111 bomber bound for Vienna. After they had arrived at a hotel in Vienna, Hitler called Skorzeny and congratulated him on the rescue, immediately awarding him the Knight's Cross and promoting him to Sturmbannführer. Hitler also tried to talk to Mussolini by phone, but after a few minutes the Duce said that he was tired and retired to his room.

The German wounded have been brought down the mountain by cable car and placed in a truck from Major Mors' column. Expecting heavy losses in the glider assault, the raiding force brought along a surgeon and a large number of medics. (Bundesarchiv, Bild 101I-567-1503-19, Fotograf: Bruno von Kayser)

---

20 Mussolini asked Mors not to punish the guard force since they had treated him well, to which Mors agreed.

Several Fallschirmjäger wave as Gerlach gets ready to take off. Skorzeny is partly visible against the rear Plexiglass. (Pier Paolo Battistelli)

While Skorzeny was winging his way to fame, Mors ordered his men to collect up equipment from the gliders, which were then set on fire (there being no way to remove them from the mountaintop). During this period the Italian troops were, peculiarly, allowed to walk freely around the area – some still armed – and inspect the German gliders. Once the raid was over, the German troops became somewhat lackadaisical and some spent nearly seven hours on the mountaintop. Mors then began ferrying Berlepsch's men, the SS men, and the Italian guards down by cable car to the Assergi station, which was completed by about 1900 hours. Campo Imperatore was left abandoned. Since it would be getting dark soon and he did not want to risk driving through possible roadblocks at night, Mors decided to bivouac his troops around the lower cable-car station in Assergi. Meanwhile, Hundt's Storch was repaired and flown back to Pratica di Mare. On the morning of September 13, Mors led the column back to Frascati, where they arrived without incident. Throughout this period, the Italian troops in L'Aquila made no move to interfere with Mors' raiding force.

A large mixed group salutes as Gerlach begins his take-off run. Schwerdt stands closest to the plane. Again, the photo indicates that at least some of the Italians were still armed. (Bundesarchiv, Bild 101I-567-1503C-37, Fotograf: Toni Schneiders)

Let the recriminations begin...

Mors spent the evening of September 12/13 discussing the raid with Berlepsch and although he was delighted that they had rescued Mussolini without any German fatalities, he was disturbed by the role played by Skorzeny. It appeared that Skorzeny had deliberately ignored Mors' entire tactical plan for the raid merely so that he could be the first to reach Mussolini. Although quiet on the mountaintop, Berlepsch now vented spleen about Skorzeny's arrogance and the poor performance of the SS men. Both men resolved to bring the issue up immediately with General Student.

Back in Germany, Himmler used the raid to demonstrate the efficiency of his SS (and thereby further discredit Admiral Canaris and his Abwehr) and German propaganda minister Josef Goebbels saw Skorzeny's exploit as a rare ray of sunshine in an otherwise gloomy season of German setbacks. Hitler willingly endorsed the aggrandizement of Skorzeny and allowed Goebbels to build him up into a Nazi super-hero. The role played by Goering's Fallschirmjäger was conveniently downplayed.

Goebbels' radio broadcasts on the morning of September 14 publicly identified Skorzeny as the organizer of the raid and the man responsible for the rescue of Mussolini. Skorzeny, interviewed on the radio, confirmed these claims and mentioned that many of the paratroopers had been killed in glider crashes. He even went on to embellish the tale with an account of a furious gun battle with the Italians, in which he emerged the victor. Other radio reports followed, referring to Skorzeny's "SS Commandos."

In Frascati, Mors was furious upon hearing these reports and immediately protested to Student, who now regretted allowing the SS to go along on the raid. Student was affronted by the lack of credit given to his Fallschirmjäger and the fabrications spouted by Skorzeny and Goebbels, but he was reluctant to take on Himmler and his SS. Instead, Student tried to work through Reichsmarshal Göring, but Göring had lost much of his stature in the Nazi hierarchy after the failure of the Stalingrad airlift and his complaints were simply ignored. However, as part of a

**SEPTEMBER 12
1943**

**1515 hours
Mussolini's plane
takes off**

As typical of the adrenaline-rush nature of intense raiding operations, many of the Fallschirmjäger quickly dozed off on the long truck ride back to Frascati. (Bundesarchiv, Bild 101I-567-1503D-21, Fotograf: Toni Schneiders)

Major Mors' column had to take all the raiding force back to Frascati, including Skorzeny's men. Here the column has paused for rest. Mors wisely decided not to try and drive back through the mountains in the dark with his tired troops. (Bundesarchiv, Bild 101I-567-1503D-25, Fotograf: Toni Schneiders)

counter-propaganda effort, Student did arrange for a film crew to visit the Gran Sasso two weeks after the raid in order to film some of his Fallschirmjäger re-enacting their role in the operation. Skorzeny and his SS men, no longer in Italy, were excluded from the film.

Student also succeeded in getting awards for the Luftwaffe participants in the raid, including several of the glider pilots, but they received them in an obscure grassy field in Italy instead of in front of the cameras in the Berliner Sportpalast, as Skorzeny's SS men did. Gerlach and Meyer-Werner both received the Ritterkreuz for their airmanship, while Mors, Berlepsch, Langguth, and three of the glider pilots received the Deutsches Kreuz in Gold (DkiG).

Four months after the Gran Sasso raid, Berlepsch was killed at Anzio and the 1 Kompanie/FJR 7 suffered a number of casualties. Mors, no longer the commander of I/FJR 7, was sent to the Eastern Front in order to silence his persistent criticisms of Skorzeny's role in the raid. In the summer of 1944, I/FJR 7 was sent to Normandy and a number of Fallschirmjäger who participated in the Gran Sasso raid were killed there. By September the remnants of the battalion had retreated into Belgium, but most were captured in the Mons pocket.

By early 1945 there was virtually no one left to contradict the official Nazi version of the Gran Sasso raid and Skorzeny's role in Operation *Greif* during the Ardennes offensive – including a false claim that he intended to assassinate General Eisenhower – which further helped to cement Skorzeny's inflated reputation. When Skorzeny wrote his postwar memoirs he claimed that he had planned and led the raid, while virtually ignoring the role of the Fallschirmjäger. However, the Fallschirmjäger who survived – including Mors – began to dispute the accepted version of the raid. Mors

Once Mussolini was gone, Mors and Berlepsch ordered their Fallschirmjäger to gather up their equipment and get ready to leave. Here an MG-42 machine-gun team collects ammunition from one of the gliders. (Bundesarchiv, Bild 101I-567-1503C-34, Fotograf: Toni Schneiders)

Hitler greets Mussolini on his arrival at Rastenberg on September 15, 1943. Despite public professions of support, Hitler was shocked by Mussolini's haggard appearance and unwillingness to go after the men who had overthrown him. It was soon obvious that Germany's main political ally was now little more than a zombie. (Author's collection)

and a number of other Fallschirmjäger described Skorzeny's postwar memoirs as "a fairy tale" and even stated that "there were no heroes on the Gran Sasso." Student and Kesselring also attempted to set the record straight after the war. Nevertheless, most popular histories of the war – even Pulitzer Prize-winner Rick Atkinson's *The Day of Battle* (2007) – continue to accept Skorzeny's distorted version of the raid without question.

Glider no. 8, flown by Unteroffizier Ronsdorf, was affected by turbulence as it came in to land and made a hard impact with the rocky surface, which tore apart its starboard wing tip. Ronsdorf and two Fallschirmjäger were injured as a result. However, Skorzeny's postwar memoirs, which claimed that this glider was "smashed to smithereens", were clearly false. (Bundesarchiv, Bild 101I-567-1503B-20, Fotograf: Toni Schneiders)

ANALYSIS

On the surface, Operation *Oak* was an immense success, no matter who eventually got the credit. German troops had rescued Mussolini from a seemingly impregnable stronghold with no deaths in the raiding force. Major Mors had succeeded in putting together a complex plan in just a matter of hours, with a minimum of intelligence, as opposed to many better-planned raids that ended in failure. Furthermore, the raid demonstrated a glider assault capability that no other force in the world at that time could match, which helped to bolster German home front morale and forced the Allies to think about a whole new operational dimension. Instead of tactical objectives designed to support ground offensives – the typical goal of special forces raids since 1939 – the Gran Sasso raid introduced a discrete form of warfare where individual high-value targets could be the objective.

Yet despite its successful outcome, the Gran Sasso raid revealed a number of tactical deficiencies, some of which continue to plague special forces operations up to this day. Foremost, the raid indicated the difficulties in mounting a close-hold, joint operation involving different services; at times, the SS and Luftwaffe were working almost at cross-purposes and Skorzeny never really accepted his subordination to Luftwaffe authority. Command and control was further disrupted during the search phase when Hitler and Himmler continued to interfere in tactical details (to the point of personally debriefing individuals who had some information about the movements of Mussolini). Indeed, micro-management of special forces operations by national-level leaders continues to have an impact on the planning and conduct of modern-day raids.

Although Hitler awarded the Ritterkreuz to Skorzeny on the same day as the raid, Goebbels ensured that he received massive public recognition at a ceremony in the Berliner Sportpalast on October 3, 1943. (Bundesarchiv, Bild 183-J07994)

The Gran Sasso raid also indicates the paramount importance of getting up-to-date and accurate information prior to committing a raiding force against a given objective. German efforts to gain information about the target succeeded only in acquiring the barest details about the hotel, and were even less successful concerning the landing zones, the size of the guard force, or the status of Mussolini. Indeed, the pre-raid reconnaissance – which Skorzeny orchestrated – was inadequate and amateurish. No real effort was made to confirm the presence of the target just before the raid, even though experience should have taught Skorzeny that the Italians had twice whisked Mussolini away before the Germans could mount an operation. While the open terrain around the hotel mitigated against any kind of large-scale ground assault, Skorzeny had three days prior to the raid in which he could have infiltrated a small team equipped with a radio and binoculars on to one of the nearby ridgelines to observe the target. Clandestine insertion of small recon teams had been used before by the Brandenbergers, but apparently this was just one more area that Skorzeny's skimpy Friedenthal training program had neglected.

Skorzeny's assertion that he ordered his men not to fire unless he fired first also flies in the face of previous German experience in glider assaults. In each case, German troops had been under fire immediately upon landing and Fallschirmjäger were trained in assault tactics, not negotiation. The fact that the Germans intended to use lethal force from the outset to squash any Italian resistance was demonstrated by the actions on contact of Mors' ground column: immediate and heavy automatic-weapons fire, followed up with grenades. Berlepsch also opted to take machine guns, light mortars, and an anti-tank gun with him on the gliders, indicating a predilection for firepower. Had Berlepsch's group landed first, as in the plan, his assault platoon would almost certainly have mowed down Faiola and his guard detail in a hail of automatic-weapons fire, blasted the furniture barricade with grenades, and then demanded that those inside the hotel surrender. Although some might argue that

SEPTEMBER 12 1943

1615 hours Mussolini arrives at Pratica di Mare and is sent on to Vienna

SEPTEMBER 12 1943

1900 hours Campo Imperatore abandoned

Berlepsch also brought a Panzerjäger team with a 2.8cm sPzB 41 tapered-bore anti-tank gun to the Gran Sasso. The 139kg weapon is mounted on wheels and pulled by ropes. The Fallschirmjäger went into battle as heavily armed as possible, realizing that they could expect no reinforcements. Note that at least three men are armed with the FG-42 assault rifle. (Bundesarchiv, Bild 101I-567-1503B-09, Fotograf: Toni Schneiders)

Some of Skorzeny's men were also decorated for the Gran Sasso raid in the Berliner Sportpalast. From right to left, Obersturmführer Ulrich Menzel, Untersturmführer Otto Schwerdt, Unterscharführer Hans Holzer, Untersturmführer Robert Warger, Hauptscharführer Manns and Unterscharführer Bernhard Cieslewitz. The two officers received the DkiG, while the enlisted men received iron crosses. Menzel's award is particularly odd given that he spent virtually the entire raid on his back with a broken ankle. (Bundesarchiv, Bild 183-J07989, Fotograf: Schwahn)

Skorzeny's approach avoided useless bloodshed, this was due only to a collapse of Italian resolve. If the Italians at Gran Sasso had resisted as their comrades did at Monterotondo, Skorzeny and Schwerdt would have been either gunned down or taken hostage. By crash-landing and moving toward the hotel with only a couple of men, Skorzeny threatened to squander the advantage of surprise and possibly encourage Italian resistance if they had realized how few Germans were initially outside the hotel.

Skorzeny's antics along the back side of the hotel are almost comical, first unable to find an entrance, then unable to get up a small platform without help. Although his memoirs make no mention of it, it also seems likely that he ran into some of Gueli's police dogs that were chained to the rear of the hotel, which would explain why it took him so long to get to the front entrance. It is clear that Skorzeny had no idea about the layout of the hotel, even though Berlepsch knew not only where the entrance was located but also about the underground tunnel that led to the upper cable-car station. Once he managed to get to the entrance, Skorzeny lost his initial boldness and only cautiously moved in when it became apparent that the Italians were not resisting. The inclusion of General Soleti proved of negligible value in the operation. It is also clear that Skorzeny's SS men performed poorly in the raid and it begs the question why only he and Schwerdt were directly involved in Mussolini's rescue. Menzel was incapacitated, but the other 13 played only minor roles in the raid even though they were among the first to land.

One of the worst aspects of the conduct of the raid was that a good extraction plan was junked merely to suit Skorzeny's personal ambition. While spotty radio contact (communication snafus are another bane of special forces operations) with Student's

headquarters made it problematic to arrange for an immediate pickup from L'Aquila, it is hard to see why Mors agreed to risk Mussolini's life in an overloaded plane. Indeed, communication with Student was re-established shortly afterwards. In later years, Mors complained a great deal about Skorzeny's behavior, but he was in a position to put a stop to these self-centered actions by refusing to allow him to jeopardize Gerlach's take-off. Instead, Mors caved in. Given his record with the Gestapo, it is not hard to imagine the kind of threats that an SD man like Skorzeny might have made to get his way. Again, the fact that Gerlach succeeded in getting both Skorzeny and Mussolini off the Campo Imperatore intact should not obscure the fact that it was a stupid move.

Finally, the Gran Sasso Raid vividly demonstrates the roles of innovation, flexibility, friction, and luck in raiding operations. Since it was impossible to mount a conventional attack upon the Gran Sasso without alerting the defenders, Student decided upon the risky method of glider assault. No one had ever attempted this under such difficult terrain and weather conditions and, by daring, the Fallschirmjäger achieved complete surprise. Even against a more resolute foe, this attack would have stunned the defenders with its audacity. However, the frictions of war weigh particularly heavily upon special operations, where even tiny changes can seriously disrupt the outcome. Berlepsch planned for 12 gliders to carry 108 of his troops, but he ended up getting only eight gliders to carry 72 of his men, plus Skorzeny's 16-man detachment. Unlike the American Colonel Charlie Beckwith, who proved inflexible in adjusting his force when he suffered unexpected helicopter losses during Operation *Eagle Claw* in 1980, Berlepsch rolled with the punches and adapted to the new circumstances so that he could complete his mission. Langguth's unplanned maneuver near Tivoli also seriously upset the entire order of landing, which could have compromised the mission. The raiders were also extremely lucky in three regards: that nine of ten glider pilots succeeded in landing intact, that the Italian guards did not take advantage of the disarray in the assault force, and that Mussolini was not executed in the first confusing moments of the raid. Indeed, luck continues to play a greater role in special operations than in conventional ones.

Mussolini has just entered the rear seat of the Storch. He does not appear very happy with this arrangement and is shocked to find out that Skorzeny will squeeze in behind him. Mussolini criticized Skorzeny for hazarding his life with this risky, overweight take-off but was ignored. (Bundesarchiv, Bild 183-J22932, Fotograf: Bruno von Kayser)

CONCLUSION

Although the Germans succeeded in rescuing Mussolini, Hitler's assumption that he could use him to rebuild Fascist Italy proved to be false. Indeed, when Mussolini was brought to Rastenberg on September 15, after the raid, Hitler was shocked to see that the Duce was a sick and broken man, without any fight left in him. While Hitler wanted him to ruthlessly hunt down the conspirators who had overthrown him in July, Mussolini expressed little interest in revenge. Nevertheless, Hitler pressed him to return to Italy and establish a Fascist alternative to the pro-Allied Badoglio government that was installed in Brindisi. Reduced to the role of a minor ally and totally dependent upon the Germans, Mussolini established the Italian Social Republic (RSI) at Salo in northern Italy only 11 days after his rescue. Mussolini did succeed in rallying some troops to his cause and by late 1944 he had about 50,000 troops in four German-trained divisions, which played a minor role in the final battles of 1944–45. Yet the RSI was little more than a puppet state that helped the Germans to maintain order in northern Italy and Mussolini knew that his days as an independent leader were over. One of the biggest impacts of Mussolini's resurrection was that it allowed the Gestapo to go after Italy's Jews, who had been off limits prior to Mussolini's ousting. Both Kappler and Gueli (now working as Mussolini's chief of security in the RSI) played major roles in the round-up of Italian Jews.

The Gran Sasso raid was a major coup for Himmler, who used it to justify creating his own parachute battalions, independent of the Luftwaffe. Only a month after the raid, the 500.SS-Fallschirmjägerbattalion was hurriedly put together. Himmler hoped to repeat the success of the Gran Sasso raid by using this unit to mount a combined parachute/glider assault on Marshal Tito's headquarters near Drvar on May 25, 1944 (Operation *Rösselsprung*). Skorzeny was involved in the initial planning and search for Tito, but it was soon clear that he was in over his head and had no idea how to plan a glider assault. Instead, Skorzeny managed to bow out before the mission was conducted and then blamed its failure on the Abwehr and the Brandenbergers. Unlike Gran Sasso, the SS paratroops failed to achieve surprise and the raid was badly botched, resulting in failure and the virtual destruction of the unit. Although the SS parachute battalion was rebuilt and later served under Skorzeny in the Ardennes, the SS never developed the kind of special forces capability that had already been created in the elite Luftwaffe Fallschirmjäger battalions.

Another result of the Gran Sasso raid was that Himmler succeeded in discrediting Admiral Canaris' Abwehr, which was finally absorbed into the RSHA in February 1944. Even the elite Brandenburg troops were brought under SD control, who then decided that their special-operations capabilities were no longer needed. Instead, the Brandenbergers were formed into a standard infantry division and sent to the Eastern Front, just as the Fallschirmjäger units were reduced to a strictly conventional role. Some Brandenbergers succeeded in transferring to Skorzeny's enlarged command and participated in Operation *Greif* in the Ardennes, which followed the style of a classic Brandenburg infiltration operation. However, the politicization of German intelligence collection and special operations essentially destroyed the Wehrmacht's ability to repeat the type of successes that it had achieved at Fort Eben Emael and the Gran Sasso.

BIBLIOGRAPHY

Primary Sources

Oberleutnant Johannes Heidenreich, *Gefechtsbericht über den Einsatz der Sonderstaffel Heidenreich am 12.9.43*

SS Officer Records, RG 242, National Archives and Research Administration

SS Enlisted BDC Records, RG 242, National Archives and Research Administration

Secondary Sources

Annussek, Greg, *Hitler's Raid to Save Mussolini*, Da Capo Press, Cambridge, MA (2005)

Davis, Melton S., *Who Defends Rome? The Forty-five Days, July 25 to September 8, 1943*, The Dial Press, New York (1972)

Eyre, Lieutenant Colonel Wayne D., *Operation Rösselsprung and the Elimination of Tito, May 25, 1944: A Failure in Planning and Intelligence Support*, Journal of Slavic Military Studies, Vol. 19 (June 2006), pp. 343–76.

Friedrich, Andreas, *Zur Befreiung Mussolinis 1943*, Der Freiwillige (September 1994)

Götzel, Herman, *Generaloberst Kurt Student und seine Fallschirmjäger: die Erinnerungen des Generaloberst Kurt Student*, Podzun-Pallas-Verlag, Friedberg (1980)

Lopez, Oscar Gonzalez, *Fallschirmjäger at the Gran Sasso*, AF Editions, Valladolid (2006)

Mussolini, Rachele, *Mussolini: An Intimate Biography by his Widow*, William Morrow & Co., New York (1974)

Patricelli, Marco, *Liberate Il Duce: Gran Sasso 1943*, Mondadori, Milan (2001)

Petacco, Arrigo and Zavoli, Sergio, *Dal Gran Consiglio al Gran Sasso: Una Storia da rifare*, Rizzoli, Milan (1973)

Radl, Karl, *Die Blitzbefreiung Mussolinis: Mit Skorzeny am Gran Sasso*, Pour le Mérite, Selent (1996)

A rain-soaked Mussolini speaking with members of one of the paramilitary "Black Brigades" in late 1944. Although the Gran Sasso raid saved Mussolini, it proved to be only a stay of execution, and when the end came he had fewer than a dozen loyal troops left. Mussolini was captured and executed by Italian partisans on April 28, 1945. (Bundesarchiv, Bild 101I-316-1181-11, Fotograf: Vack)

INDEX

References to illustrations are shown in **bold**.